JAMES MADISON'S
"Advice to My Country"

JAMES MADISON'S
"Advice to My Country"

Edited by
DAVID B. MATTERN

UNIVERSITY PRESS OF VIRGINIA
Charlottesville and London

University of Virginia Press
© 1997 by the Rector and Visitors of the University of Virginia
Printed in the United States of America on acid-free paper

First published 1997
First paperback edition published 2013
ISBN 978-0-8139-3492-1 (paper)

1 3 5 7 9 8 6 4 2

THE LIBRARY OF CONGRESS HAS CATALOGED THE HARDCOVER EDITION AS
FOLLOWS:

Library of Congress Cataloging-in-Publication Data
Madison, James, 1751–1836.
   James Madison's "Advice to my country" / edited by David B. Mattern.
      p.   cm.
   Includes index.
   ISBN 0-8139-1717-4
   1. United States—Politics and government—1775–1783—Quotations,
maxims, etc.   2. United States—Politics and government—1783–1815—
Quotations, maxims, etc.   3. Madison, James, 1751–1836—Quotations.
I. Mattern, David B., 1951– . II. Title.
   E302.M192 1997
   973.5'1–dc20
                                                           96-28149
                                                              CIP

CONTENTS

Contents

ACKNOWLEDGMENTS

My first thanks must go to Mary Katherine Hassett, who suggested the idea of this book, and to Dick Holway, whose indefatigable efforts made sure it survived. Thanks are also due their colleague at the University Press of Virginia, designer Janet Anderson.

I owe a special debt of gratitude to John Stagg, who encouraged the project from the start, read the manuscript, and offered timely advice, and to Peter Onuf, whose detailed suggestions made this a greatly improved book. My thanks to Bernadette McCauley for her insightful comments on the introduction. Anonymous readers also generously reviewed the proposal for which I am grateful. I thank my colleagues at The Papers of James Madison — Jeanne Cross, Susan Perdue, Mary Hackett, and Jewel Spangler — for their suggestions and encouragement, and all the past editors of the project for keeping the quote file current.

Finally, this book is dedicated to my son Ben and his generation, who, I hope, will cherish the political legacy they inherit from James Madison; and to my wife, Charlotte Crystal, to whom I am indebted beyond the power of words to tell.

Repository Symbols and Short Titles

DLC	Library of Congress
DNA	National Archives
Ketcham, *James Madison*	Ralph Ketcham, *James Madison: A Biography* (1971; rept. Charlottesville, Va., 1990)
MiU-C	William L. Clements Library, Ann Arbor, Mich.
MHi	Massachusetts Historical Society, Boston
NjP	Princeton University, Princeton, N.J.
PCarlD	Dickinson College, Carlisle, Pa.
PJM	*The Papers of James Madison*, Congressional Series
PJM-SS	*The Papers of James Madison, Secretary of State Series*
PJM-PS	*The Papers of James Madison, Presidential Series*

CHRONOLOGY

INTRODUCTION

JAMES MADISON was a small man whose quiet voice was often drowned out by the hubbub of a legislative assembly. Yet his words—as preserved in his speeches, essays, and letters—resound across the centuries with an authority unmatched by any other man of his generation. Americans may turn to Thomas Jefferson for inspiration, to Benjamin Franklin for wit and charm, and to George Washington for steadfast courage in the face of overwhelming odds, but when questions involve the structure and workings of their government, they invariably seek out Madison. Lawyers and judges read him to guide their thinking on constitutional matters. Pundits and politicians frequently cite the Virginian to bolster their arguments and "get right with the Founders."

Why is Madison preeminent among those who fought the American Revolution and established a new nation? His undisputed authority on the broad questions of American government comes from his key role as a leading member of the Constitutional Convention, contributing author to *The Federalist*, and leading legislator in the First Federal Congress. The U.S. Constitution—that masterpiece of separated powers and checks and balances which governed in Madison's time and still governs in our own—bears the stamp of Madison's mind more than of any other Founder. That in itself would be cause enough to pay heed to his words.

Yet, in addition, he served the public for forty years—in the Virginia General Assembly, the Continental Congress, the Constitutional Convention, the Federal Congress, as secretary of state, and as president of the United States—and he lived another twenty years through a productive retirement, reflecting on his service and the republican government instituted by himself and his colleagues. He left his fellow Americans down through the centuries a legacy of thoughtful, well-researched speeches, letters, and essays on public issues. In short, we read Madison because he still matters.

James Madison was not a great orator in the mold of Patrick Henry. Nor did his presence command a room in the way George Washington's could. Rather, Madison won the respect and admiration of his peers by being the best-prepared speaker on any public issue. As a contemporary noted, Madison "blends together the profound politician with the scholar. . . . From a spirit of industry and application which he possesses in a most eminent degree, he always comes forward the best informed man of any point in debate" (Ralph Ketcham, *James Madison: A Biography* [1971; rept. Charlottesville, Va., 1990], p. 201). This was no accident. Madison spent many lonely hours poring over dusty volumes of history, researching the past to illuminate the present. He often burned candle after candle during long nights reading and writing at his desk. The fruits of that labor could be seen in his speeches as Madison tried to persuade the opposition, not with emotional flights of oratory, but with the luminous light of reason and a realistic understanding of the nature of man.

Recognition of James Madison's seminal role in establishing the United States has grown dramatically over the past forty years. Long obscured by the fame of his brilliant friend, Thomas Jefferson, Madison has emerged as an intellectual giant in his own right. Interest in Madison, particularly as the "Father of the Constitution," grew as a result of the edicts of an activist Supreme Court in the 1950s and 1960s, renewed interest in the American Revolution and the Early Republic years during the Bicentennial celebrations, and the debate over the meaning of "original intent" that began in earnest during the Reagan presidency and continues to this day.

Scholarly interest in Madison also grew apace in this period, with the launching of a new edition of Madison's papers as well as publication of a score of books on various aspects of his life. *The Papers of James Madison*, which now has published twenty-three of a prospective fifty-four volumes, including all the material pertaining to the Founding years, provides complete and authoritative texts of Madison's writings and has played no small part in the resurgence of interest in the fourth president.

This is as it should be. James Madison reflected and wrote about American political life and government for more than sixty years and in the process grappled with questions of human nature and politics that transcend time. Can a representative government govern effectively and still preserve the people's rights? What role should religion play in public life? What are the proper limits of executive and legislative power? What role should the state play in achieving and maintaining an educated populace? What are the proper boundaries between federal and state governments? Should the freedom of the press be absolute? What should be the role of the United States in world affairs? On these topics and more, Madison had many thoughtful and thought-provoking things to say.

And he said them well. Madison wrote with precision, clarity, and subtlety, though he was not a phrasemaker like Jefferson. The difference is instructive. Hugh Blair Grigsby, who knew Madison in old age, compared the two friends this way: "Force and point and rapid analysis are the characteristics of the style of Jefferson; full, clear, and deliberate disquisition carefully wrought out, as if the writer regarded himself rather as the representative of truth than the exponent of the doctrines of party or even a nation, is the praise of Madison" (ibid., pp. 472–73). Jefferson often sounded one bold bright note, as in a stirring trumpet solo, whereas Madison used the full orchestral range to explore ideas in all their shades of meaning and intricate reasoning. What he suffers in comparison with Jefferson's epigramatic style, Madison makes up for in the depth and logic of his thought.

These extracts from Madison's writings contain little of a personal nature. He destroyed most of his private correspondence in retirement as he compiled and edited his public papers. His wife, Dolley Payne Madison, also may have burned many of his personal letters after his death. But what little evidence survives, coupled with anecdotal evidence from those who visited the Madisons or knew them intimately, belies the conventional portrait of Madison as merely awkward and stiff. Certainly he was an intensely private man who often appeared cold and bookish and at times was "too much the disputatious pleader," in the words of British diplomat Augustus John Foster (ibid., p. 428). In public he often seemed shy and ill at ease. At his first inaugural ball, for example, Margaret Bayard Smith wrote that Madison wore a "most woe begone face," and mentioned to one guest that he wished he was home in bed (ibid., pp. 475–76). But to his intimates and the countless visitors he welcomed into the family circle at Montpelier or in Washington he was "a social, jovial and good-humored companion full of anecdote," with a penchant for telling ribald stories (ibid., p. 428). If little of this amiable and earthy Madison is apparent in this volume, it is because he suppressed that side of his personality to present himself as a model republican leader.

What is apparent, however, is Madison's tough-minded, unsentimental view of his fellow man and of politics as the art of the possible. Man is capable of virtuous action in Madison's thought but almost always pursues his own self-interest. How then can man be entrusted with governing himself in a republican world? Madison's solution was to build the elegant and complex machinery of the federal government, designed to check and circumscribe power in ways that over the long term would preserve the greatest share of liberty for its citizens. Madison was always concerned with constructing and administering a "compound" republic, consisting of both national and state governments, that would preserve and protect the rights of individuals and property while at the same time advancing a reasoned and democratically accepted conception of the public good (in the broadest sense of that term). Madison acknowledged that this balance of power and rights would be extraordinarily difficult to maintain when he wrote, "What is government itself but the greatest of all reflections on human nature? If men were angels, no government would be necessary" (*PJM* 10:477). It was not a government designed for a perfect world; it was merely the best possible government yet devised.

The Constitution that Madison fathered left a great evil relatively untouched: slavery. That Madison considered it a curse is true. That the fruits of the "peculiar institution" supported him throughout all his days in the lavish style known to the Virginia gentry is also true. That he could hold these two parts of the slavery equation in balance throughout his life illustrates one aspect of the tragedy of race relations in America and the tenacious grip with which it still holds us in thrall. The selections on slavery and African Americans are the saddest in the book.

Deeply painful as slavery was (and as the memory of it is still today), it should not deter Americans from all walks of life from considering Madison's legacy their own. For the plantation owner of Montpelier was also the man who worried and struggled within Congress to pass the Bill of Rights, that "parchment barrier" on which so many of our personal rights are founded. Without Madison's indefatigable efforts in the First Federal Congress, freedoms that we take for granted—such as the right to speak, worship, and associate as we please—would not be enjoyed by Americans. As a reflection of Madison's deep concern for the interpretation of the U.S. Constitution, this book includes a great number of entries under constitutional topics.

There was nothing that Madison believed in more strongly throughout his long life than his conviction that people should be free to profess, or not to profess, the religion of their choice. His belief in the separation of church and state was ironclad and can be found in his earliest exchange of letters with his college friend William Bradford; when he was fighting for complete liberty of conscience at his first legislative assembly in 1776; when he drafted a "Memorial and Remonstrance against Religious Assessments" in 1785; and on numerous occasions during his retirement when he commented on various books and pamphlets sent to him. The extracts published here represent a position from which Madison never retreated.

There are few entries for the years from 1801 to 1817, when Madison served as President Jefferson's secretary of state (1801–9) and as president (1809–17). The press of executive business during those years, which included the waging of a war with Great Britain, was so great that Madison virtually suspended his private correspondence. As he concentrated on affairs of state, he had little time to devote to philosophical discourse, and his personal letters became shorter and confined to business. After he retired, however, he returned to his writing desk with relish, eager to explain and defend his contributions to the founding and early years of the infant United States.

As a youth Madison, like many of his contemporaries, kept a commonplace book, a notebook in which he jotted down selections from writers that instructed, pleased, or provoked him and to which he occasionally added a comment or two. Madison's surviving commonplace book is interesting for a number of reasons, including the indications it gives us of the wide range of his reading and interests in his formative years.

This collection of Madison's writings is a kind of commonplace book. It is designed as a ready reference to Madison's thought, including his most perceptive observations on government and human nature. As a representative sample of his writings—in breadth and depth—it should be useful to journalists, politicians, and policymakers, as well as the general reader. Culled from the roughly six thousand known items that Madison wrote, the selections provide inspiration, guidance, instruction, and a window into the mind of one of our greatest Founders.

The texts were taken from the published volumes of *The Papers of James Madison*, where available, and from copies of the original manuscripts, when not. After every entry is a source line that will facilitate further investigation of its context. The detailed index makes a search for related selections quick and easy. All insertions within brackets are my own and have been added to clarify or provide context for an otherwise obscure reference. With two exceptions—the spelling out of such abbreviations as "wh" for "which," "Xian" for "Christian," and so on, and the correction of misspellings—the excerpts are rendered exactly as Madison wrote them. They are presented in hopes that readers will be intrigued and stimulated by them and that they will turn to the published volumes of the Madison Papers to pursue in greater depth the thinking of the "great little Madison."

P R O L O G U E

My life has been so much a public one, that any review of it
must mainly consist of the agency which was my lot in public
transactions; and of that agency the portions probably most ac-
ceptable to general curiosity, are to be found in my manuscript
preservations of some of those transactions, and in the epistolary
communications to confidential friends, made at the time and on
the spot, whilst I was a member of political Bodies General, or
Local. My judgment has accorded with my inclination, that any
publicity of which selections from this miscellany may be thought
worthy, should await a posthumous date.

To James K. Paulding, April 1831
DLC: Madison Papers

JAMES MADISON'S
"Advice to My Country"

John Adams

The answers of Mr. Adams to his addressors form the most gro-
tesque scene in the tragi-comedy acting by the Government. . . .
He is verifying completely the last feature in the character drawn
of him by Dr. F[ranklin] however his title may stand to the two
first. "Always an honest man, often a wise one, but sometimes
wholly out of his senses."

> To Thomas Jefferson, 10 June 1798
> *PJM* 17:150

That he had a mind rich in ideas of its own, as well as in its
learned store; with an ardent love of Country, and the merit of
being a colossal champion of its Independence, must be allowed
by those most offended by the alloy in his Republicanism, and
the fervors and flights originating in his moral temperament.

> To James K. Paulding, April 1831
> DLC: Madison Papers

Affliction

Afflictions of every kind are the onerous conditions charged on
the tenure of life; and it is a silencing if not a satisfactory vindi-
cation of the ways of Heaven to Man, that there are but few
who do not prefer an acquiescence in them, to a surrender of
the tenure itself.

> To John G. Jackson, 28 Dec. 1821
> DLC: Madison Papers

African Americans

I am glad to find the legislature persist in their resolution to re-
cruit their line of the army for the war, though without deciding
on the expediency of the mode under their consideration, would
it not be as well to liberate and make soldiers at once of the
blacks themselves as to make them instruments for enlisting
white Soldiers? It would certainly be more consonant to the

principles of liberty which ought never to be lost sight of in a contest for liberty, and with white officers and a majority of white soldiers no imaginable danger could be feared from themselves, as there certainly could be none from the effect of the example on those who should remain in bondage: experience having shown that a freedman immediately loses all attachment and sympathy with his former fellow slaves.

To Joseph Jones, 28 Nov. 1780
PJM 2:209

On a view of all circumstances I have judged it most prudent not to force Billey back to Virginia even if [it] could be done; and have accordingly taken measures for his final separation from me. I am persuaded his mind is too thoroughly tainted to be a fit companion for fellow slaves in Virginia. The laws here do not admit of his being sold for more than 7 years. I do not expect to get near the worth of him; but cannot think of punishing him by transportation merely for coveting that liberty for which we have paid the price of so much blood, and have proclaimed so often to be the right, and worthy the pursuit, of every human being.

To James Madison, Sr., 8 Sept. 1783
PJM 7:304

Agriculture

In my opinion, it would be proper also, for gentlemen to consider the means of encouraging the great staple of America, I mean agriculture, which I think may justly be styled the staple of the United States; from the spontaneous productions which nature furnishes, and the manifest preference it has over every other object of emolument in this country.

Speech in Congress, 9 Apr. 1789
PJM 12:71

The life of the husbandman is pre-eminently suited to the comfort and happiness of the individual. *Health*, the first of blessings, is an appurtenance of his property and his employment. *Virtue,* the health of the soul, is another part of his patrimony, and no less favored by his situation. *Intelligence* may be cultivated in this as well as in any other walk of life. If the mind be less susceptible of polish in retirement than in a crowd, it is more capable of profound and comprehensive efforts. Is it more ignorant of some things? It has a compensation in its ignorance of others. *Competency* is more universally the lot of those who dwell in the country, when liberty is at the same time their lot. The extremes both of want and of waste have other abodes.

> *National Gazette* essay, 3 Mar. 1792
> *PJM* 14:245

The class of citizens who provide at once their own food and their own raiment, may be viewed as the most truly independent and happy. They are more: they are the best basis of public liberty, and the strongest bulwark of public safety. It follows, that the greater the proportion of this class to the whole society, the more free, the more independent, and the more happy must be the society itself.

> *National Gazette* essay, 3 Mar. 1792
> *PJM* 14:246

I thank you most cordially for the invitation to your hospitable mansion, but I can not promise myself the benefit of it. In my relaxation, from this place [Washington, D.C.], I am obliged to keep in mind that I am a farmer, and am willing to flatter myself, that my farm will be the better for my presence.

> To Horatio Gates, 10 Mar. 1802
> *PJM-SS* 3:19

The first and most useful of the Arts.

> To John S. Skinner, 14 Apr. 1829
> DLC: Madison Papers

Ambition

Ambition is so vigilant, and where it has a model always in view as in the present case, is so prompt in seizing its advantages, that it can not be too closely watched, or too vigorously checked.

To Thomas Jefferson, 25 Dec. 1797
PJM 17:63

America and the World

Is it not the glory of the people of America, that whilst they have paid a decent regard to the opinions of former times and other nations, they have not suffered a blind veneration for antiquity, for custom, or for names, to overrule the suggestions of their own good sense, the knowledge of their own situation, and the lessons of their own experience? To this manly spirit, posterity will be indebted for the possession, and the world for the example of the numerous innovations displayed on the American theatre, in favour of private rights and public happiness.

The Federalist No. 14, 30 Nov. 1787
PJM 10:288

All Europe must by degrees be aroused to the recollection and assertion of the rights of human nature. Your good will to Mankind will be gratified with this prospect, and your pleasure as an American be enhanced by the reflection that the light which is chasing darkness and despotism from the old world, is but an emanation from that which has procured and succeeded the establishment of liberty in the New.

To Edmund Pendleton, 4 Mar. 1790
PJM 13:86

The U.S. are now furnishing models and lessons to all the world, a great, soon to be the most hopeful portion of it, is receiving them with a happy docility; whilst the great European portion is either passively or actively gaining by them. The eyes of the world being thus on our Country, it is put the more on its good behaviour, and under the greater obligation also, to do justice to

the Tree of Liberty by an exhibition of the fine fruits we gather
from it.

To James Monroe, 16 Dec. 1824
DLC: Monroe Papers

American Politics

A government, deriving its energy from the will of the society,
and operating by the reason of its measures, on the understanding and interest of the society. Such is the government for which
philosophy has been searching, and humanity been sighing,
from the most remote ages. Such are the republican governments which it is the glory of America to have invented, and her
unrivalled happiness to possess.

National Gazette essay, 18 Feb. 1792
PJM 14:234

Here [in the United States], we are, on the whole, doing well,
and giving an example of a free system, which I trust will be
more of a pilot to a good port, than a Beacon, warning from a
bad one. We have, it is true, occasional fevers; but they are of
the transient kind, flying off through the surface, without prey-
ing on the vitals. A Government like ours has so many safety-
valves, giving vent to overheated passions, that it carries within
itself a relief against the infirmities from which the best of human Institutions can not be exempt.

To Lafayette, 25 Nov. 1820
DLC: Madison Papers

American Revolution

The fundamental principle of the revolution was, that the colo-
nies were co-ordinate members with each other, and with Great-
Britain; of an Empire, united by a common Executive Sovereign,
but not united by any common Legislative Sovereign. The Legislative power was maintained to be as complete in each American Parliament, as in the British Parliament. And the royal

prerogative was in force in each colony, by virtue of its acknowledging the King for its Executive Magistrate, as it was in Great-Britain, by virtue of a like acknowledgment there. A denial of these principles by Great-Britain, and the assertion of them by America, produced the revolution.

The Report of 1800, 7 Jan. 1800
PJM 17:327

The assertion by Great Britain of a power to make laws for the other members of the Empire *in all cases whatsoever*, ended in the discovery, that she had a right to make laws for them, *in no cases whatsoever*.

The Report of 1800, 7 Jan. 1800
PJM 17:328

And although among our blessings we cannot number an exemption from the evils of war; yet these will never be regarded as the greatest of evils by the friends of liberty and of the rights of nations. Our country has before preferred them to the degraded condition which was the alternative, when the sword was drawn in the cause which gave birth to our national Independence, and none who contemplate the magnitude, and feel the value of that glorious event, will shrink from a struggle to maintain the high and happy ground on which it placed the American people.

Annual Message to Congress,
7 Dec. 1813
DNA: Record Group 233, President's
Messages

The infant periods of most nations are buried in silence or veiled in fable; and the world perhaps has lost but little which it needs regret. The origin and outset of the American Republic contain lessons of which posterity ought not to be deprived: and happily there never was a case in which every interesting incident could be so accurately preserved.

To William Eustis, 6 July 1819
DLC: Madison Papers

Appeasement

It will not easily be supposed, that a refusal to part with our rights without an equivalent; will be made the pretext of a war on us: much less that such a pretext will be founded on our refusal to mingle a sacrifice of our commerce and navigation, with an adjustment of political differences: Nor is any evidence to be found either in History or Human Nature, that nations, are to be bribed out of a spirit of encroachment and aggression, by humiliations which nourish their pride, or by concessions which extend their resources and power.

> Petition to the Virginia General
> Assembly, September 1795
> *PJM* 16:76

Appointment Power

The appointment to offices is, of all the functions of Republican and perhaps every other form of Government, the most difficult to guard against abuse. Give it to a numerous body, and you at once destroy all responsibility, and create a perpetual source of faction and corruption. Give it to the Executive wholly, and it may be made an engine of improper influence and favoritism.

> Observations on Jefferson's Draft
> Constitution, 15 Oct. 1788
> *PJM* 11:290

The dispensation to office, tho' among the most important, is likewise among the most simple of public duties. One solitary principle governs every case: "That the man appointed to an office shall be irreproachable in point of morality, and in other respects well qualified to discharge its duties with credit to himself and advantage to his country." The most ordinary capacity may comprehend the principle, and know what should be done. Talents of the more elevated kind are only requisite to enable those trustees of this portion of the public confidence, in the range of faculties, judiciously to distinguish between men, and to select those best suited for the stations to which they shall be destined. To apply, in short, the most expedient means for the attainment of given ends. If appointments, from the highest to the lowest grade, will bear the test of enquiry by this criterion, those who confer them may rest contented: they have nothing to apprehend from the reproach of their own consciences, or the censure of the public.

> *Dunlap's American Daily Advertiser* essay,
> 20 Oct. 1792
> *PJM* 14:388–89

Argument

A bad cause seldom fails to betray itself.

> *The Federalist* No. 41, 19 Jan. 1788
> *PJM* 10:394

Arts

Regarding the Arts which it [the Society of Artists of Philadelphia] cherishes, as among the endowments and enjoyments, which characterize human Society, under its highest and happiest destinies; it is one of my ardent wishes, that the tendency of our free system of Government may be portrayed as well in what may contribute to embellish the mind and refine the manners, as in those primary blessings, of which it already affords so many grateful proofs and presages.

> To Benjamin Henry Latrobe and George
> Murray, 28 Jan. 1811
> *PJM-PS* 3:139

Support for the Arts and Sciences

Well aware as I am, that public bodies are liable to be assailed by visionary projectors, I nevertheless wish to ascertain the probability of the magnetic theory. If there is any considerable probability that the projected voyage would be successful, or throw any valuable light on the discovery of longitude, it certainly comports with the honor and dignity of government to give it their countenance and support. Gentlemen will recollect, that some of the most important discoveries, both in arts and sciences, have come forward under very unpromising and suspicious appearances.

Speech in Congress, 20 Apr. 1789
PJM 12:92

Astronomy

Every insight into the grandeur and structure of the universe, having a happy tendency at once to expand the human mind, and to cherish its moral conceptions, astronomy in its most simple and intelligible developments, must always form a useful element in popular Education.

To Ferdinand R. Hassler, 6 Mar. 1828
DLC: Madison Papers

Balance of Powers

But the great security against a gradual concentration of the several powers in the same department, consists in giving to those who administer each department, the necessary constitutional means, and personal motives, to resist encroachments of the others. The provision for defence must in this, as in all other cases, be made commensurate to the danger of attack. Ambition must be made to counteract ambition. The interest of the man must be connected with the constitutional rights of the place. It may be a reflection on human nature, that such devices should be necessary to control the abuses of government. But what is government itself but the greatest of all reflections on human nature? If men were angels, no government would be necessary. If angels were to govern men, neither external nor internal controls on government would be necessary. In framing a government which is to be administered by men over men, the great difficulty lies in this: You must first enable the government to control the governed; and in the next place, oblige it to control itself. A dependence on the people is no doubt the primary control on the government; but experience has taught mankind the necessity of auxiliary precautions.

The Federalist No. 51, 6 Feb. 1788
PJM 10:477

Banks

With regard to Banks, they have taken too deep and too wide a root in social transactions, to be got rid of altogether, if that were desirable. In providing a convenient substitute, to a certain extent, for the metallic currency, and a fund of credit, which prudence may turn to good account, they have a hold on public opinion, which alone would make it expedient to aim rather at the improvement, than the suppression of them. As now generally constituted, their advantages whatever they be, are outweighed by the excesses of their paper emissions, and the partialities and corruption with which they are administered.

To James K. Paulding, 10 Mar. 1827
DLC: Rives Collection, Madison Papers

The Bill of Rights

What use then it may be asked can a bill of rights serve in popular Governments? I answer the two following which though less essential than in other Governments, sufficiently recommend the precaution. 1. The political truths declared in that solemn manner acquire by degrees the character of fundamental maxims of free Government, and as they become incorporated with the national sentiment, counteract the impulses of interest and passion. 2. Altho' it be generally true as above stated that the danger of oppression lies in the interested majorities of the people rather than in usurped acts of the Government, yet there may be occasions on which the evil may spring from the latter sources; and on such, a bill of rights will be a good ground for an appeal to the sense of the community.

To Thomas Jefferson, 17 Oct. 1788
PJM 11:298–99

In proportion as Government is influenced by opinion, must it be so by whatever influences opinion. This decides the question concerning a bill of rights, which acquires efficacy as time sanctifies and incorporates it with the public sentiment.

> Notes for Essays,
> 19 Dec. 1791–3 Mar. 1792
> *PJM* 14:162–63

In Europe, charters of liberty have been granted by power. America has set the example and France has followed it, of charters of power granted by liberty. This revolution in the practice of the world, may, with an honest praise, be pronounced the most triumphant epoch of its history, and the most consoling presage of its happiness.

> *National Gazette* essay, 18 Jan. 1792
> *PJM* 14:191

Books

With us [in the United States] there are more readers than buyers of Books. In England there are more buyers than Readers. Hence those Gorgeous Editions, which are destined to sleep in the private libraries of the Rich, whose vanity aspires to that species of furniture; or who give that turn to their public spirit and patronage of letters.

> To Edward Everett, 19 Mar. 1823
> DLC: Madison Papers

City Life

'Tis not the country that peoples either the Bridewells or the Bedlams. These mansions of wretchedness are tenanted from the distresses and vices of overgrown cities.

> *National Gazette* essay, 3 Mar. 1792
> *PJM* 14:245

Civil Liberty

In a free government, the security for civil rights must be the same as that for religious rights. It consists in the one case in the multiplicity of interests, and in the other, in the multiplicity of sects.

> *The Federalist* No. 51, 6 Feb. 1788
> *PJM* 10:478–79

As a man is said to have a right to his property, he may be equally said to have a property in his rights. Where an excess of power prevails, property of no sort is duly respected. No man is safe in his opinions, his person, his faculties, or his possessions.

> *National Gazette* essay, 27 Mar. 1792
> *PJM* 14:266

Commerce

Wherever Commerce prevails there will be an inequality of wealth, and wherever the latter does a simplicity of manners must decline.

> To Edmund Randolph, 30 Sept. 1783
> *PJM* 7:363

I own myself the friend to a very free system of commerce, and hold it as a truth, that commercial shackles are generally unjust, oppressive and impolitic—it is also a truth, that if industry and labour are left to take their own course, they will generally be directed to those objects which are the most productive, and this in a more certain and direct manner than the wisdom of the most enlightened legislature could point out.

> Speech in Congress, 9 Apr. 1789
> *PJM* 12:71

Common Law

If it be understood that the common law is established by the constitution, it follows that no part of the law can be altered by the legislature . . . and the whole code with all its incongruities, barbarisms, and bloody maxims would be inviolably saddled on the good people of the United States.

The Report of 1800, 7 Jan. 1800
PJM 17:331–32

Confederation

I have not yet found leisure to scan the project of a Continental Convention with so close an eye as to have made up any observations worthy of being mentioned to you. In general I hold it for a maxim that the Union of the States is essential to their safety against foreign danger, and internal contention; and that the perpetuity and efficacy of the present system can not be confided on. The question therefore is, in what mode and at what moment the experiment for supplying the defects ought to be made.

To Richard Henry Lee, 25 Dec. 1784
PJM 8:201

Is it possible with such an example before our eyes of impotency in the federal system, to remain sceptical with regard to the necessity of infusing more energy into it? A Government cannot long stand which is obliged in the ordinary course of its administration to court a compliance with its *constitutional* acts, from a member not of the most powerful order, situated within the immediate verge of authority, and apprized of every circumstance which should remonstrate against disobedience. The question whether it be possible and worthwhile to preserve the Union of the States must be speedily decided some way or other. Those who are indifferent to its preservation would do well to look forward to the consequences of its extinction. The prospect to my eye is a gloomy one indeed.

To James Monroe, 9 Apr. 1786
PJM 9:25

A sanction is essential to the idea of law, as coercion is to that of Government. The federal system [under the Articles of Confederation] being destitute of both, wants the great vital principles of a Political Constitution. Under the form of such a Constitution, it is in fact nothing more than a treaty of amity of commerce and of alliance, between so many independent and Sovereign States. From what cause could so fatal an omission have happened in the articles of Confederation? from a mistaken confidence that the justice, the good faith, the honor, the sound policy, of the several legislative assemblies would render superfluous any appeal to the ordinary motives by which the laws secure the obedience of individuals: a confidence which does honor to the enthusiastic virtue of the compilers, as much as the inexperience of the crisis apologizes for their errors.

"Vices of the Political System,"
April 1787
PJM 9:351

Conflict of Interest

No dividend on Stock of the U.S. can belong to me. On my first entrance into public life, I formed a resolution from which I never departed, to abstain, whilst in that situation from dealing in any way, in public property or transactions of any kind; and I am satisfied that during my respites, and since my retirement, from the public Service, I never became possessed of any Stock that could give me a title to the derelict in question.

To Anthony Morris, 27 Jan. 1826
DLC: Madison Papers

Whilst a member of the House of Representatives he forbore to follow the example, to which he believes he was the sole exception, of receiving at the public expense the Articles of Stationery provided for the members, to which he thought he was no more entitled, than to the supply of other wants incident to his station. To this resolution he adhered throughout, tho' without attracting any notice to it that might lead to a reflection on others. On his first entering public life, he had laid down strict rules for himself in pecuniary matters—one invariably observed was, never to deal in public property, lands, debts or money, whilst a member of the body whose proceedings might influence these transactions.

Madison's Autobiography, 1831
DLC: Madison Papers

Congress

I have observed, that gentlemen suppose, that the general legislature will do every mischief they possibly can, and that they will omit to do every thing good which they are authorised to do. If this were a reasonable supposition, their objections would be good. I consider it reasonable to conclude, that they will as readily do their duty, as deviate from it: Nor do I go on the grounds mentioned by gentlemen on the other side—that we are to place unlimited confidence in them, and expect nothing but the most exalted integrity and sublime virtue. But I go on this great republican principle, that the people will have virtue and intelligence to select men of virtue and wisdom. Is there no virtue among us? If there be not, we are in a wretched situation. No theoretical checks—no form of government can render us secure. To suppose that any form of government will secure liberty or happiness without any virtue in the people, is a chimerical idea. If there be sufficient virtue and intelligence in the community, it will be exercised in the selection of these men. So that we do not depend on their virtue, or put confidence in our rulers, but in the people who are to choose them.

Speech in the Virginia Ratifying
Convention, 20 June 1788
PJM 11:163

Mr. Madison thought it an important principle, and one that ought in general to be attended to—That all laws should be made to operate as much on the law makers as upon the people; the greatest security for the preservation of liberty, is for the government to have a sympathy with those on whom the laws act, and a real participation and communication of all their burthens and grievances. Whenever it is necessary to exempt any part of the government from sharing in these common burthens, that necessity ought not only to be palpable, but should on no account be exceeded.

Speech in Congress, 16 Dec. 1790
PJM 13:323

Conscience

Conscience is the most sacred of all property; other property depending in part on positive law, the exercise of that, being a natural and unalienable right. To guard a man's house as his castle, to pay public and enforce private debts with the most exact faith, can give no title to invade a man's conscience which is more sacred than his castle, or to withhold from it that debt of protection, for which the public faith is pledged, by the very nature and original conditions of the social pact.

National Gazette essay, 27 Mar. 1792
PJM 14:267

Conscientious Objection

But there is a question of great magnitude, which I am desirous of having determined. I shall therefore take the liberty of moving it: That we add to the end of the amendment, the words, "and persons conscientiously scrupulous of bearing arms" [be exempt from militia service]. I agree with the gentleman who was last up, that [it] is the glory of this country, the boast of the revolution, and the pride of the present constitution, that here the rights of mankind are known and established on a basis more certain, and I trust, more durable, than any heretofore recorded in history, or existing in any other part of this globe; but above all, it is the particular glory of this country, to have secured the rights of conscience which in other nations are least understood or most strangely violated.

Speech in Congress, 22 Dec. 1790
PJM 13:328

Consistency

I am neither so blind nor so vain as to claim an entire exemption from the changes of opinion, or from the argumentative inaccuracies and inconsistencies, incident to a very long course of political life; and to a participation in a great variety of political discussions, under many vicisitudes and varying aspects of the subjects of them. A comparative exemption is as much as I dare aspire to; and this I ought to presume will not be refused, if I should be found to have a title to it.

To Tench Coxe, 17 Jan. 1821
DLC: Madison Papers

For, altho' far from regarding a change of opinion under the lights of experience and the results of improved reflection as exposed to censure, and still farther from the vanity of supposing myself less in need than others of that privilege, I had indulged the belief that there were few, if any, of my co-temporaries, thro' the long period and varied services of my political life, to whom a mutability of opinion on great Constitutional questions was less applicable.

To Nicholas P. Trist, December 1831
DLC: Madison Papers

Consolidation

Here then is a proper object presented, both to those who are most jealously attached to the separate authority reserved to the states, and to those who may be more inclined to contemplate the people of America in the light of one nation. Let the former continue to watch against every encroachment, which might lead to a gradual consolidation of the states into one government. Let the latter employ their utmost zeal, by eradicating local prejudices and mistaken rivalships, to consolidate the affairs of the states into one harmonious interest; and let it be the patriotic study of all, to maintain the various authorities established by our complicated system, each in its respective constitutional sphere; and to erect over the whole, one paramount Empire of reason, benevolence and brotherly affection.

National Gazette essay, 3 Dec. 1791
PJM 14:139

U.S. Constitution

The great objects which presented themselves were 1. to unite a proper energy in the Executive and a proper stability in the Legislative departments, with the essential characters of Republican Government. 2. to draw a line of demarkation which would give to the General Government every power requisite for general purposes, and leave to the States every power which might be most beneficially administered by them. 3. to provide for the different interests of different parts of the Union. 4. to adjust the clashing pretensions of the large and small States. Each of these objects was pregnant with difficulties. The whole of them together formed a task more difficult than can be well conceived by those who were not concerned in the execution of it. Adding to these considerations the natural diversity of human opinions on all new and complicated subjects, it is impossible to consider the degree of concord which ultimately prevailed as less than a miracle.

To Thomas Jefferson, 24 Oct. 1787
PJM 10:207–8

The diversity of opinions on so interesting a subject [the Constitution], among men of equal integrity and discernment, is at once a melancholy proof of the fallibility of the human judgment, and of the imperfect progress yet made in the science of Government.

To Archibald Stuart, 30 Oct. 1787
PJM 10:232

You ask me why I agreed to the Constitution proposed by the Convention at Philadelphia? I answer, because I thought it safe to the liberties of the people, and the best that could be obtained from the jarring interests of States, and the miscellaneous opinions of Politicians; and because experience has proved that the real danger to America and to liberty lies in the defect of *energy and stability* in the present establishments of the United States.

To Philip Mazzei, 8 Oct. 1788
PJM 11:278

The happy union of these States is a wonder: their Constitution a miracle: their example the hope of Liberty throughout the World. Woe to the ambition that initiates the destruction of either.

Notes on the Federal Constitution,
September 1829
DLC: Madison Papers

The Constitution of the United States being established by a competent authority, by that of the sovereign people of the several States who were the parties to it; it remains only to enquire what the Constitution is; and here it speaks for itself: It organizes a Government into the usual Legislative, Executive and Judiciary Departments; invests it with specified powers, leaving others to the parties to the Constitution; it makes the Government like other Governments to operate directly on the people; it places at its command the needful physical means of executing its powers; and finally proclaims its supremacy and that of the laws made in pursuance of it, over the Constitution and laws of the States; the powers of the Government being exercised, as in other elective and responsible Governments, under the control of its Constituents the people and the Legislatures of the States; and subject to the Revolutionary rights of the people in extreme cases. Such is the Constitution of the United States de jure and de facto; and the name whatever it may be, that may be given to it, can make it nothing more or less than what it actually is.

To Daniel Webster, 15 Mar. 1833
DLC: Madison Papers

You give me a credit to which I have no claim in calling me "*The* writer of the Constitution of the U.S." This was not, like the fabled Goddess of Wisdom, the offspring of a single brain. It ought to be regarded as the work of many heads and many hands.

To William Cogswell, 10 Mar. 1834
DLC: Madison Papers

Constitutional Amendments

The danger of disturbing the public tranquility by interesting too strongly the public passions, is a still more serious objection against a frequent reference of constitutional questions, to the decision of the whole society. Notwithstanding the success which has attended the revisions of our established forms of government, and which does so much honor to the virtue and intelligence of the people of America, it must be confessed, that the experiments are of too ticklish a nature to be unnecessarily multiplied.

The Federalist No. 49, 2 Feb. 1788
PJM 10:462

It may be considered as an objection inherent in the principle, that as every appeal to the people would carry an implication of some defect in the government, frequent appeals would in great measure deprive the government of that veneration which time bestows on every thing, and without which perhaps the wisest and freest governments would not possess the requisite stability. If it be true that all governments rest on opinion, it is no less true that the strength of opinion in each individual, and its practical influence on his conduct, depend much on the number which he supposes to have entertained the same opinion. The reason of man, like man himself, is timid and cautious, when left alone; and acquires firmness and confidence, in proportion to the number with which it is associated. When the examples, which fortify opinion, are *ancient* as well as *numerous*, they are known to have a double effect. In a nation of philosophers, this consideration ought to be disregarded. A reverence for the laws, would be sufficiently inculcated by the voice of an enlightened reason. But a nation of philosophers is as little to be expected as the philosophical race of kings wished for by Plato. And in every other nation, the most rational government will not find it a superfluous advantage to have the prejudices of the community on its side.

The Federalist No. 49, 2 Feb. 1788
PJM 10:461–62

The Constitution of the United States may doubtless disclose from time to time, faults which call for the pruning or the ingrafting hand. But remedies ought to be applied, not in the paroxysms of party and popular excitements; but with the more leisure and reflection, as the Great Departments of power according to experience may be successively and alternately in and out of public favour; and as changes hastily accommodated to these vicissitudes would destroy the symmetry and the stability aimed at in our political system.

To John M. Patton, 24 Mar. 1834
DLC: Madison Papers

Constitutional Conventions

The danger of disturbing the public tranquility by interesting too strongly the public passions, is a still more serious objection against a frequent reference of constitutional questions, to the decision of the whole society. . . . We are to recollect that all the existing constitutions were formed in the midst of a danger which repressed the passions most unfriendly to order and concord; of an enthusiastic confidence of the people in their patriotic leaders, which stifled the ordinary diversity of opinions on great national questions; of a universal ardor for new and opposite forms, produced by a universal resentment and indignation against the ancient government; and whilst no spirit of party, connected with the changes to be made, or the abuses to be reformed, could mingle its leaven in the operation. The future situations in which we must expect to be usually placed, do not present any equivalent security against the danger which is apprehended.

The Federalist No. 49, 2 Feb. 1788
PJM 10:462

Constitutional Interpretation

No axiom is more clearly established in law, or in reason, than that wherever the end is required, the means are authorised; wherever a general power to do a thing is given, every particular power necessary for doing it, is included.

The Federalist No. 44, 25 Jan. 1788
PJM 10:424

The federal Government has been hitherto limited to the Specified powers, by the greatest Champions for Latitude in expounding those powers. If not only the *means*, but the *objects* are unlimited, the parchment had better be thrown into the fire at once.

To Henry Lee, 1 Jan. 1792
PJM 14:180

If Congress can do whatever in their *discretion* can be *done by money*, and will promote the *general welfare*, the Government is no longer a limited one possessing enumerated powers, but an indefinite one subject to particular exceptions. It is to be remarked that the phrase out of which this doctrine is elaborated, is copied from the old articles of Confederation, where it was always understood as nothing more than a general caption to the specified powers, and it is a fact that it was preferred in the new instrument for that very reason as less liable than any other to misconstruction.

To Edmund Pendleton, 21 Jan. 1792
PJM 14:195–96

If Congress can apply money indefinitely to the general welfare, and are the sole and supreme judges of the general welfare, they may take the care of religion into their own hands; they may establish teachers in every state, county, and parish, and pay them out of the public treasury; they may take into their own hands the education of children, establishing in like manner schools throughout the union; they may assume the provision for the poor; they may undertake the regulation of all roads other than post roads; in short, every thing, from the highest object of state legislation, down to the most minute object of police, would be thrown under the power of Congress; for every object I have mentioned would admit the application of money, and might be called, if Congress pleased, provisions for the general welfare.

Speech in Congress, 6 Feb. 1792
PJM 14:223

I, sir, have always conceived—I believe those who proposed the constitution conceived; it is still more fully known, and more material to observe, those who ratified the constitution conceived, that this is not an indefinite government deriving its powers from the general terms prefixed to the specified powers—but, a limited government tied down to the specified powers, which explain and define the general terms.

Speech in Congress, 6 Feb. 1792
PJM 14:221

It would be absurd to say, first, that Congress may do what they please; and then, that they may do this or that particular thing. After giving Congress power to raise money, and apply it to all purposes which they may pronounce necessary to the general welfare, it would be absurd, to say the least, to superadd a power to raise armies, to provide fleets, &c. In fact, the meaning of the general terms in question must either be sought in the subsequent enumerations which limits and details them, or they convert the government from one limited as hitherto supposed, to the enumerated powers, into a government without any limits at all.

Speech in Congress, 6 Feb. 1792
PJM 14:221

But, after all, whatever veneration might be entertained for the body of men who formed our constitution, the sense of that body could never be regarded as the oracular guide in the expounding the constitution. As the instrument came from them, it was nothing more than the draught of a plan, nothing but a dead letter, until life and validity were breathed into it, by the voice of the people, speaking through the several state conventions. If we were to look therefore, for the meaning of the instrument, beyond the face of the instrument, we must look for it not in the general convention, which proposed, but in the state conventions, which accepted and ratified the constitution.

Speech in Congress, 6 Apr. 1796
PJM 16:295–96

So far is the political system of the United States distinguishable from that of other countries, by the caution with which powers are delegated and defined; that in one very important case, even of commercial regulation and revenue, the power is absolutely locked up against the hands of both governments. A tax on exports can be laid by no Constitutional authority whatever.

The Report of 1800, 7 Jan. 1800
PJM 17:323

Serious danger seems to be threatened to the genuine sense of the Constitution, not only by an unwarrantable latitude of construction, but by the use made of precedents which can not be supposed to have had in the view of their authors, the bearing contended for, and even where they may have crept thro' inadvertence, into acts of Congress, and been signed by the Executive at a midnight hour, in the midst of a group scarcely admitting perusal, and under a weariness of mind as little admitting a vigilant attention. Another and perhaps a greater danger is to be apprehended from the influence which the usefulness and popularity of measures may have on questions of their constitutionality.

To James Monroe, 27 Dec. 1817
DLC: Monroe Papers

What is of most importance [in the decision of *McCulloch* v. *Maryland*] is the high sanction given to a latitude in expounding the Constitution which seems to break down the landmarks intended by a specification of the powers of Congress, and to substitute for a definite connection between means and ends, a Legislative discretion as to the former to which no practical limit can be assigned. In the great system of political economy having for its general object the national welfare, every thing is related immediately or remotely to every other thing; and consequently a power over any one thing, if not limited by some obvious and precise affinity, may amount to a power over every other. Ends and means may shift their character at the will and according to the ingenuity of the Legislative Body. . . . It could not but happen, and was foreseen at the birth of the Constitution, that difficulties and differences of opinion might occasionally arise in expounding terms and phrases, necessarily used in such a Charter, more especially those which divide legislation between the General and local Governments; and that it might require a regular course of practice, to liquidate and settle the meaning of some of them. But it was anticipated I believe by few if any of the friends of the Constitution, that a rule of construction would be introduced as broad and as pliant as what has occurred.

> To Spencer Roane, 2 Sept. 1819
> DLC: Madison Papers

I entirely concur in the propriety of resorting to the sense in which the Constitution was accepted and ratified by the nation. In that sense alone it is the legitimate Constitution. And if that be not the guide in expounding it, there can be no security for a consistent and stable, more than for a faithful exercise of its powers. If the meaning of the text be sought in the changeable meaning of the words composing it, it is evident that the shape and attributes of the Government must partake of the changes to which the words and phrases of all living languages are constantly subject. What a metamorphosis would be produced in the code of law if all its ancient phraseology were to be taken in its modern sense. And that the language of our Constitution is already undergoing interpretations unknown to its founders, will I believe appear to all unbiassed Enquirers into the history of its origin and adoption.

To Henry Lee, 25 June 1824
DLC: Madison Papers

Corporations

There is an evil which ought to be guarded against in the indefinite accumulation of property from the capacity of holding it in perpetuity by ecclesiastical corporations. The power of all corporations, ought to be limited in this respect. The growing wealth acquired by them never fails to be a source of abuses.

Detached Memoranda, *post* 1817
DLC: Rives Collection, Madison Papers

Incorporated Companies, with proper limitations and guards, may in particular cases, be useful, but they are at best a necessary evil only. Monopolies and perpetuities are objects of just abhorrence. The former are unjust to the existing, the latter usurpations on the rights of future generations. Is it not strange that the Law which will not permit an individual to bequeath his property to the descendants of his own loins for more than a short and strictly defined term, should authorize an associated few, to entail perpetual and indefeasable appropriations; and that, not only to objects visible and tangible, but to particular opinions, consisting, sometimes, of the most metaphysical niceties; as is the case with Ecclesiastical Corporations.

To James K. Paulding, 10 Mar. 1827
DLC: Rives Collection, Madison Papers

Credit

The experience of European Merchants who have speculated in our trade will probably check in a great measure our opportunities of consuming beyond our resources; but they will continue to credit us as far as our coin in addition to our productions will extend, and our experience here teaches us that our people will extend their consumption as far as credit can be obtained.

To James Monroe, 9 Apr. 1786
PJM 9:25-26

Criticism of the Government

It must be seen that no two principles can be either more indefensible in reason, or more dangerous in practice—than that 1. arbitrary denunciations may punish, what the law permits, & what the Legislature has no right, by law, to prohibit—and that 2. the Government may stifle all censures whatever on its misdoings; for if it be itself the Judge it will never allow any censures to be just, and if it can suppress censures flowing from one lawful source it may those flowing from any other—from the press and from individuals as well as from Societies.

To James Monroe, 4 Dec. 1794
PJM 15:407

A Cure for All Ills

Let me recommend the best medicine in the world: a long journey, at a mild Season, thro' a pleasant Country, in easy stages.

To Horatio Gates, 23 Feb. 1794
PJM 15:264-65

Death

Nothing more than a change of *mind*, my dear.

Madison's last words, 28 June 1836
As quoted in Ketcham, *Madison*, p. 670

Debate

When I alluded to the proceedings of this day [in Congress], I contemplated the *manner* in which the business was conducted;

and though I acknowledge that a majority ought to govern, yet they have no authority to deprive the minority of a constitutional right; they have no authority to debar us the right of free debate. An important and interesting question being under consideration, we ought to have time allowed for its discussion. Facts have been stated on one side, and members ought to be indulged on the other with an opportunity of collecting and ascertaining other facts. We have a right to bring forward all the arguments which we think can, and ought to have an influence on the decision.

Speech in Congress, 3 Sept. 1789
PJM 12:372

He [Madison] was sorry that it almost always happened, whenever any question of general policy and advantage to the union was before the House, when gentlemen found themselves at a loss for general arguments, they commonly resorted to local views; and at all times as well as the present, when there was most occasion for members to act with the utmost coolness, when their judgments ought to be the least biassed—it was to be regretted that at those times they suffered their feelings, passions and prejudices to govern their reason. Thus it is that the most important points are embarrassed, the northern and southern interests are held up, every local circumstance comes into view, and every idea of liberality and candor is banished.

Speech in Congress, 19 Dec. 1791
PJM 14:171

Deficit

I think it would be a powerful and unanswerable objection against assuming the state debts at this time, that we do not see or are not prepared to decide on the means of providing for them. There is not a more important and fundamental principle in legislation, than that the ways and means ought always to face the public engagements; that our appropriations should ever go hand in hand with our promises. To say that the United States should be answerable for twenty-five millions of dollars without knowing whether the ways and means can be provided, and without knowing whether those who are to succeed us will think with us on the subject, would be rash and unjustifiable. Sir, in my opinion, it would be hazarding the public faith in a manner contrary to every idea of prudence.

Speech in Congress, 22 Apr. 1790
PJM 13:173

Diet

Horticulture is a valuable and interesting Section of Agriculture, the main resource of human subsistence. Apart from the ornamental, the scientific, and experimental uses, which it may embrace, it affords a cheap and wholesome substitute for the disproportionate consumption of animal food, which has long been a habit of our Country, resulting from the exuberant supply it has enjoyed of this article. In promoting a reform of this habit, horticultural Societies can not fail of a happy tendency.

To George Watterson, 8 Mar. 1824
DLC: Madison Papers

Diplomacy

It is a nice task to speak of war, so as to impress our own people with a dislike of it, and not impress foreign Governments with the idea that they may take advantage of the dislike.

To Thomas Jefferson, 7 Sept. 1808
DLC: Jefferson Papers

District of Columbia

If any state had the power of legislation over the place where congress should fix the general government; this would impair the dignity, and hazard the safety of congress. If the safety of the union were under the control of any particular state, would not

foreign corruption probably prevail in such a state, to induce it
to exert its controlling influence over the members of the general government?

> Speech in the Virginia Ratifying
> Convention, 6 June 1788
> *PJM* 11:81

Distrust of Government

Complaints are every where heard from our most considerate
and virtuous citizens, equally the friends of public and private
faith, and of public and personal liberty; that our governments
are too unstable; that the public good is disregarded in the conflicts of rival parties; and that measures are too often decided,
not according to the rules of justice, and the rights of the minor
party; but by the superior force of an interested and over-
bearing majority. . . . It will be found indeed, on a candid review
of our situation, that some of the distresses under which we labour, have been erroneously charged on the operation of our
governments; but it will be found at the same time, that other
causes will not alone account for many of our heaviest misfor-
tunes; and particularly, for that prevailing and increasing distrust
of public engagements, and alarm for private rights, which are
echoed from one end of the continent to the other. These must
be chiefly, if not wholly, effects of the unsteadiness and injustice,
with which a factious spirit has tainted our public administration.

> *The Federalist* No. 10, 22 Nov. 1787
> *PJM* 10:264

Drugs and Alcohol

A *compleat* suppression of every species of stimulating indulgence, if attainable at all, must be a work of peculiar difficulty,
since it has to encounter not only the force of habit, but a propensity in human nature. In every age and nation, some exhilarating or exciting substance seems to have been sought for, as a

relief from the languor of idleness, or the fatigues of labor. In the rudest state of Society, whether in hot or cold climates, a passion for ardent spirits is in a manner universal. In the progress of refinement, beverages less intoxicating, but still of an exhilarating quality, have been more or less common. And where all these sources of excitement have been unknown, or been totally prohibited by a religious faith, substitutes have been found in opium, in the nut of the betel, the root of the Ginseng, or the leaf of the Tobacco plant.

It would doubtless be a great point gained for our Country . . . if ardent spirits could be made only to give way to malt liquors, to those afforded by the apple and the pear, and to the lighter and cheaper varieties of wine. It is remarkable that in the Countries where the grape supplies the common beverage, habits of intoxication are rare; and in some places almost without example.

To Thomas Hertell, 20 Dec. 1819
DLC: Madison Papers

Education

Whilst it is universally admitted that a well instructed people alone, can be permanently a free people; and whilst it is evident that the means of diffusing and improving useful knowledge, form so small a proportion of the expenditures for national purposes, I cannot presume it to be unseasonable, to invite your attention to the advantages of superadding, to the means of Education provided by the several States, a Seminary of Learning, instituted by the national Legislature, within the limits of their exclusive jurisdiction; the expence of which might be defrayed, or reimbursed, out of the vacant grounds which have accrued to the Nation, within those limits. Such an Institution, tho' local in its legal character, would be universal in its beneficial effects. By enlightening the opinions, by expanding the patriotism; and by assimilating the principles, the sentiments and the manners of those who might resort to this Temple of Science, to be redistributed, in due time, through every part of the community; sources of jealousy and prejudice would be diminished, the features of national character would be multiplied, and greater extent given to Social harmony. But above all, a well constituted Seminary, in the center of the nation, is recommended by the consideration, that the additional instruction emanating from it, would contribute not less to strengthen the foundations, than to adorn the structure, of our free and happy system of Government.

Annual Message to Congress,
5 Dec. 1810
PJM-PS 3:52

Learned Institutions ought to be favorite objects with every free people. They throw that light over the public mind which is the best security against crafty and dangerous encroachments on the public liberty. They are nurseries of skillful Teachers for the schools distributed throughout the Community. They are themselves Schools for the particular talents required for some of the public Trusts, on the able execution of which the welfare of the people depends. They multiply the educated individuals from among whom the people may elect a due portion of their public agents of every description; more especially of those who are to frame the laws; by the perspicuity, the consistency, and the stability, as well as by the just and equal spirit of which the great social purposes are to be answered. . . . What spectacle can be more edifying or more seasonable, than that of Liberty and Learning, each leaning on the other for their mutual and surest support?

To William T. Barry, 4 Aug. 1822
DLC: Madison Papers

Your old friend Mr. Jefferson still lives, and will close his illustrious career, by bequeathing to his Country a Magnificent Institute for the advancement and diffusion of Knowledge, which is

the only Guardian of true liberty, the great cause to which his
life has been devoted.

To George Thomson, 30 June 1825
NjP

I congratulate you on the foundation thus laid for a general System of Education, and hope it presages a superstructure, worthy of the patriotic forecast which has commenced the Work. The best service that can be rendered to a Country, next to that of giving it liberty, is in diffusing the mental improvement equally essential to the preservation, and the enjoyment of the blessing.

To Littleton Dennis Teackle,
29 Mar. 1826
DLC: Madison Papers

No feature in the aspect of our Country is more gratifying, than the increase and variety of Institutions for educating the several ages and classes of the rising generation, and the meritorious patriotism which improving on their most improved forms extends the benefit of them to the sex heretofore, sharing too little of it. Considered as at once the fruits of our free System of Government, and the true means of sustaining and recommending it, such establishments are entitled to the best praise that can be offered.

To Gulian C. Verplanck, 14 Feb. 1828
DLC: Madison Papers

Elections

In the election of Delegates to the Legislature for the ensuing year (1777), he was an unsuccessful candidate. Previous to the Revolution the election of the County Representatives, was as in England, septennial, and it was as there the usage for the Candidates to recommend themselves to the voters, not only by personal solicitation, but by the corrupting influence of spirituous liquors, and other treats, having a like tendency. Regarding these as equally inconsistent with the purity of moral and of republican principles; and anxious to promote, by his example, the proper reform, he trusted to the new views of the subject which he hoped would prevail with the people; whilst his competitors adhered to the old practice. The consequence was that the election went against him; his abstinence being represented as the effect of pride or parsimony.

Madison's Autobiography, 1831
DLC: Madison Papers

An auxiliary desideratum for the melioration of the Republican form is such a process of elections as will most certainly extract from the mass of the Society the purest and noblest characters which it contains; such as will at once feel most strongly the proper motives to pursue the end of their appointment, and be most capable to devise the proper means of attaining it.

"Vices of the Political System,"
April 1787
PJM 9:357

I am now pressed by some of my friends to repair to Virginia as a requisite expedient for counteracting the machinations against my election into the House of Representatives. To this again I am extremely disinclined for reasons additional to the one above mentioned. It will have an electioneering appearance which I always despised and wish to shun.

To Edmund Randolph, 23 Nov. 1788
PJM 11:363

The Executive

The constitution supposes, what the History of all Governments demonstrates, that the Executive is the branch of power most interested in war, and most prone to it.

To Thomas Jefferson, 2 Apr. 1798
PJM 17:104

I cannot feel all the alarm you express at the prospect for the future, as reflected from the mirror of the past. It will be a rare

case that the Presidential contest will not issue in a choice that
will not discredit the Station, and not be acquiesced in by the
unsuccessful party, foreseeing as it must do, the appeal to be
again made at no very distant day, to the will of the nation. As
long as the Country shall be exempt from a Military force powerful in itself, and combined with a powerful faction, liberty and
peace will find safeguards in the Elective resource, and the spirit
of the people.

To James Hillhouse, 17 May 1830
DLC: Madison Papers

Faction

The latent causes of faction are thus sown in the nature of man;
and we see them every where brought into different degrees of
activity, according to the different circumstances of civil society.
A zeal for different opinions concerning religion, concerning
government, and many other points, as well of speculation as of
practice; an attachment to different leaders ambitiously con-
tending for pre-eminence and power; or to persons of other de-
scriptions whose fortunes have been interesting to the human
passions, have in turn divided mankind into parties, inflamed
them with mutual animosity, and rendered them much more disposed to vex and oppress each other, than to co-operate for their
common good.

The Federalist No. 10, 22 Nov. 1787
PJM 10:265

Within the local limits, parties generally exist, founded on the
different sorts of property, even sometimes on divisions by
streets or little streams; frequently on political and religious differences. Attachments to rival individuals, are not seldom a
source of the same divisions. In all these cases, the party animosities are the more violent as the compass of the Society may
more easily admit of the contagion and collision of the passions;

and according to that violence is the danger of oppression by one party on the other; by the majority on the minority.

Detached Memoranda, *post* 1817
DLC: Rives Collection, Madison Papers

Fashion

Can any despotism be more cruel than a situation, in which the existence of thousands depends on one will, and that will on the most slight and fickle of all motives, a mere whim of the imagination.

National Gazette essay, 20 Mar. 1792
PJM 14:258

Federalism

In the American Constitution The general authority will be derived entirely from the subordinate authorities. The Senate will represent the States in their political capacity; the other House will represent the people of the States in their individual capacity. The former will be accountable to their constituents at moderate, the latter at short periods. The President also derives his appointment from the States, and is periodically accountable to them. This dependence of the General, on the local authorities, seems effectually to guard the latter against any dangerous encroachments of the former: Whilst the latter, within their respective limits, will be continually sensible of the abridgment of their power, and be stimulated by ambition to resume the surrendered portion of it. We find the representatives of Counties and corporations in the Legislatures of the States, much more disposed to sacrifice the aggregate interest, and even authority, to the local views of their Constituents: than the latter to the former. I mean not by these remarks to insinuate that an esprit de corps will not exist in the national Government or that opportunities may not occur, of extending its jurisdiction in some points. I mean only that the danger of encroachments is much greater from the other side, and that the impossibility of dividing powers of legislation, in such a manner, as to be free from different constructions by different interests, or even from ambiguity in the judgment of the impartial, requires some such expedient as I contend for.

To Thomas Jefferson, 24 Oct. 1787
PJM 10:210–11

That this Assembly doth explicitly and peremptorily declare, that it views the powers of the federal government, as resulting from the compact to which the states are parties; as limited by the plain sense and intention of the instrument constituting that compact; as no farther valid than they are authorised by the grants enumerated in that compact, and that in case of a deliberate, palpable and dangerous exercise of other powers not granted by the said compact, the states who are parties thereto have the right, and are in duty bound, to interpose for arresting the progress of the evil, and for maintaining within their respective limits, the authorities, rights and liberties appertaining to them.

Virginia Resolutions, 21 Dec. 1798
PJM 17:189

My prolonged life has made me a witness of the alternate popularity, and unpopularity of each of the great branches of the Federal Government. I have witnessed, also, the vicissitudes, in the apparent tendencies in the Federal and State Governments, to encroach each on the authorities of the other, without being able to infer with certainty, what would be the final operation of the causes as heretofore existing; whilst it is far more difficult to calculate, the mingled and checkered influences, on the future from an expanding territorial Domain: from the multiplication of the parties to the Union, from the great and growing power of not a few of them, from the absence of external danger; from combinations of States in some quarters, and collisions in others, and from questions, incident to a refusal of the unsuccessful party to abide by the issue of controversies judiciously decided. To these uncertainties, may be added, the effects of a dense population and the multiplication, and the varying relations of the classes composing it. I am far however from desponding of the great political experiment in the hands of the American people.

> To an unidentified correspondent,
> March 1836
> DLC: Madison Papers

Federal Lands

You request an answer at length to the claim of the new States to the Federal lands within their limits. . . . I have always viewed the claim as so unfair and unjust, so contrary to the certain and notorious intentions of the parties to the case, and so directly in the teeth of the condition on which the lands were ceded to the Union, that if a technical title could be made out by the claimants, it ought in conscience and honor to be waived. But the title in the people of the U.S. rests on a foundation too just and solid to be shaken by any technical or metaphysical arguments whatever.

> To Edward Coles, 28 June 1831
> DLC: Madison Papers

Federal-State Relations

Our Governmental System is established by a compact not between the Government of the United States, and the State Governments; but between the States, as sovereign communities, stipulating each with the others, a surrender of certain portions of their respective authorities, to be exercised by a Common Government, and a reservation, for their own exercise, of all their other authorities.

> To Spencer Roane, 29 June 1821
> DLC: Madison Papers

I continue to express a flattering confidence that in the midst of political conflicts and party excitements, it will ever be kept in mind, that the compound and peculiarly modified polity, under which the blessings of public Liberty, of individual Security, of internal tranquility and of general prosperity have been enjoyed in a degree and for a period having no example ancient or modern, reposes on an equilibrium of powers as constitutionally divided between the Government of the whole and the Government of its parts; that the equilibrium must be equally disturbed by an assumption by either of the Governments of powers belonging to the other; and that the entire System necessarily has for its basis, an equal and uniform validity and operation of the Acts of the Union throughout all the States composing it.

To Francis T. Brooke, 22 Feb. 1828
DLC: Madison Papers

I partake of the wonder that the men you name should view secession in the light mentioned. The essential difference between a free Government and Governments not free, is that the former is founded in compact, the parties to which are mutually and equally bound by it. Neither of them therefore can have a greater right to break off from the bargain, than the other or others have to hold them to it. And certainly there is nothing in the Virginia Resolutions of '98 adverse to this principle, which is that of common sense and common justice. The fallacy which draws a different conclusion from them lies in confounding a *single* party, with the *parties* to the Constitutional compact of the United States. The latter having made the compact may do what they will with it. The former as one only of the parties, owes fidelity to it, till released by consent, or absolved by an intolerable abuse of the power created.

To Nicholas P. Trist, 23 Dec. 1832
DLC: Madison Papers

Foreign Relations

Fear and hatred of other nations [is] the greatest cement, [and] always appealed to by rulers when they wish to impose burdens or carry unpopular points.

Notes for Essays,
19 Dec. 1791–3 Mar. 1792
PJM 14:160–61

The management of foreign relations appears to be the most susceptible of abuse, of all the trusts committed to a Government, because they can be concealed or disclosed, or disclosed in such parts and at such times as will best suit particular views; and because the body of the people are less capable of judging and are more under the influence of prejudices, on that branch of their affairs, than of any other. Perhaps it is a universal truth that the loss of liberty at home is to be charged to provisions against danger real or pretended from abroad.

To Thomas Jefferson, 13 May 1798
PJM 17:130

The fetters imposed on liberty at home have ever been forged out of the weapons provided for defence against real, pretended, or imaginary dangers from abroad.

"Political Reflections," 23 Feb. 1799
PJM 17:242

Altho' it does not accord with the general sentiments or views of the United States to intermeddle with the domestic controversies of other Countries, it cannot be unfair in the prosecution of a just war, or the accomplishment of a reasonable peace, to take advantage of the hostile cooperation of others.

To James Leander Cathcart,
22 Aug. 1802
PJM-SS 3:504

A free people, firmly united, in a just cause, can never despond of either inspiring a respect for their rights, or of maintaining them against hostile invasions.

To John Keemle, 17 Jan. 1810
PJM-PS 2:188

Benjamin Franklin

[Franklin] has written his own life: and no man had a finer one to write, or a better title to be himself the writer.

To James K. Paulding, April 1831
DLC: Madison Papers

Free Trade

The unqualified Theory of "Let us alone," presupposes a perpetual peace, and universal freedom of Commerce among Nations, making them, in certain economical respects, but one and the same Nation. A Nation that does not provide in some measure against the effect of Wars, and the policy of other Nations, on its commerce and manufactures, necessarily exposes these interests to the caprice and casualty of events. The extent and the mode of the provision proper to be made, are fair questions for examination and unavoidable sources of conflicting opinions; not to say possible sources of oppressive decisions.

To George McDuffie, 30 Mar. 1828
DLC: Madison Papers

The champions, for the "Let alone policy" forget that theories are the offspring of the Closet; exceptions and qualifications the lessons of experience.

To Charles J. Ingersoll, 30 Dec. 1835
DLC: Madison Papers

Friendship

Friendship like all Truth delights in plainess and simplicity and It is the Counterfeit alone that needs Ornament and ostentation.

To William Bradford, 28 Apr. 1773
PJM 1:83

Frugality

The want of economy in the use of imported articles, enters very justly into the explanation given of the causes of the present general embarrassments [the panic of 1819]. Were every one to live within his income or even the savings of the prudent to exceed the deficits of the extravagant, the balance in the foreign commerce of the nation, could not be against it. The want of a due economy has produced the unfavorable turn which has been experienced. . . . It has been made a question whether Banks, when restricted to spheres in which temporary loans only are made to persons in active business promising quick returns, do not as much harm to imprudent, as good to prudent borrowers. But it can no longer be a doubt with any, that loan offices, carrying to every man's door, and even courting his acceptance of the monied means of gratifying his present wishes under a prospect or hope of procrastinated repayment, must, of all devices, be the one most fatal to a general frugality, and the benefits resulting from it.

To Clarkson Crolius, December 1819
DLC: Madison Papers

God

This belief in a God All Powerful wise and good, is so essential to the moral order of the world and to the happiness of man, that arguments which enforce it cannot be drawn from too many sources nor adapted with too much solicitude to the different characters and capacities to be impressed with it. . . . The finiteness of the Human understanding betrays itself on all subjects, but more especially when it contemplates such as involve infinity. What may safely be said seems to be, that the infinity of time and space forces itself on our conception, a limitation of either being inconceivable: that the mind prefers at once the idea of a self existing cause to that of an infinite series of cause and effect, which augments, instead of avoiding the difficulty: and that it finds more facility in assenting to the self existence of an invisible cause possessing infinite power, wisdom and goodness, than to the self existence of the universe, visibly destitute of those attributes, and which may be the effect of them.

To Frederick Beasley, 29 Nov. 1825
DLC: Madison Papers

Government

The principles and Modes of Government are too important to be disregarded by an Inquisitive mind and I think are well worthy of a critical examination by all students that have health and Leisure.

To William Bradford, 1 Dec. 1773
PJM 1:101

The great desideratum in Government is, so to modify the sovereignty as that it may be sufficiently neutral between different parts of the Society to controul one part from invading the rights of another, and at the same time sufficiently controuled itself, from setting up an interest adverse to that of the entire Society.

To Thomas Jefferson, 24 Oct. 1787
PJM 10:214

Energy in government is essential to that security against external and internal danger, and to that prompt and salutary execution of the laws, which enter into the very definition of good government. Stability in government, is essential to national character, and to the advantages annexed to it, as well as to that repose and confidence in the minds of the people, which are among the chief blessings of civil society. . . . The genius of republican liberty, seems to demand on one side, not only, that all power should be derived from the people; but, that those entrusted with it should be kept in dependence on the people, by a short duration of their appointments; and, that, even during this short period, the trust should be placed not in a few, but in a number of hands. Stability, on the contrary, requires, that the hands, in which power is lodged, should continue for a length of time the same. A frequent change of men will result from a frequent return of electors, and a frequent change of measures, from a frequent change of men; whilst energy in government requires not only a certain duration of power, but the execution of it by a single hand.

> *The Federalist* No. 37, 11 Jan. 1788
> *PJM* 10:361

Governments destitute of energy, will ever produce anarchy.

> Speech in the Virginia Ratifying
> Convention, 7 June 1788
> *PJM* 11:93

There never was a government without force. What is the meaning of government? An institution to make people do their duty. A government leaving it to a man to do his duty, or not, as he pleases, would be a new species of government, or rather no government at all.

> Speech in the Virginia Ratifying
> Convention, 16 June 1788
> *PJM* 11:146

A Government of the same structure, would operate very differently within a very small territory and a very extensive one: over a people homogeneous in their opinions and pursuits, and over a people consisting of adverse sects in religion, or attached to adverse theories of Government: over a Society composed wholly of tenants of the soil aspiring and hoping for an enlargement of their possessions and a society divided into a rich or independent class, and a more numerous class without property and hopeless of acquiring a permanent interest in maintaining its rights: over a nation secure against foreign enemies, and over one in the midst of formidable neighbours.

> Notes on Government, December 1791
> PJM 14:132

The best provision for a stable and free Government is not a balance in the powers of the Government tho' that is not to be neglected, but an equilibrium in the interests and passions of the Society itself, which can not be attained in a small Society.

> Notes for Essays,
> 19 Dec. 1791–3 Mar. 1792
> PJM 14:158–59

It has been said that all Government is an evil. It would be more proper to say that the necessity of any Government is a misfortune. This necessity however exists; and the problem to be solved is, not what form of Government is perfect, but which of the forms is least imperfect.

> To an unidentified correspondent,
> ca. 1833
> DLC: Madison Papers

Alexander Hamilton

The publication [of Hamilton's pamphlet] under all its characters is a curious specimen of the ingenious folly of its author. Next to the error of publishing at all, is that of forgetting that simplicity and candor are the only dress which prudence would put on innocence. Here we see every rhetorical artifice employed to excite the spirit of party to prop up his sinking reputation, and whilst the most exaggerated complaints are uttered against the unfair and virulent persecutions of himself, he deals out in every page the most malignant insinuations, against others. The one against you is a masterpiece of folly, because its impotence is in exact proportion to its venom.

> To Thomas Jefferson, 20 Oct. 1797
> *PJM* 17:54

That he possessed intellectual powers of the first order, and the moral qualities of integrity and honor in a captivating degree, has been decreed to him by a suffrage now universal. If his Theory of Government deviated from the Republican standard, he had the candor to avow it, and the greater merit of co-operating faithfully in maturing and supporting a system which was not his choice. The criticism to which his share in the administration of it, was most liable was that it had the aspect of an effort to give to the Instrument a constructive and practical bearing not warranted by its true and intended character.

> To James K. Paulding, April 1831
> DLC: Madison Papers

History

No studies seem so well calculated to give a proper expansion to the mind as Geography and history; and when not absorbing an undue portion of time, are as beneficial and becoming to the one sex as to the other.

> To Reynolds Chapman, 25 Jan. 1821
> DLC: Madison Papers

Honesty

In a multitude of counsellors there is the best chance for honesty, if not of wisdom.

> To Edmund Randolph, 1 May 1782
> *PJM* 4:197

Impartiality

A certain degree of impartiality or the appearance of it, is necessary in the most despotic Governments. In republics, this may
be considered as the vital principle of the Administration. And in
a *federal* Republic founded on local distinctions involving local
jealousies, it ought to be attended to with a still more scrupulous exactness.

To Edmund Pendleton, 20 Oct. 1788
PJM 11:306–7

Intellectuals

The class of literati is not less necessary than any other. They
are the cultivators of the human mind—the manufacturers of
useful knowledge—the agents of the commerce of ideas—the
censors of public manners—the teachers of the arts of life and
the means of happiness.

Notes for Essays, December 1791
PJM 14:168

Interest Groups

In every political society, parties are unavoidable. A difference
of interests, real or supposed, is the most natural and fruitful
source of them. The great object should be to combat the evil:
1. By establishing a political equality among all. 2. By withhold-
ing *unnecessary* opportunities from a few, to increase the inequality of property, by an immoderate, and especially an unmerited,
accumulation of riches. 3. By the silent operation of laws, which,
without violating the rights of property, reduce extreme wealth
towards a state of mediocrity, and raise extreme indigence towards a state of comfort. 4. By abstaining from measures which
operate differently on different interests, and particularly such
as favor one interest at the expence of another. 5. By making one

party a check on the other, so far as the existence of parties cannot be prevented, nor their views accommodated. If this is not the language of reason, it is that of republicanism.

National Gazette essay, 23 Jan. 1792
PJM 14:197

Thomas Jefferson

He lives and will live in the memory and gratitude of the wise and good, as a luminary of science, as a votary of liberty, as a model of patriotism, and as a benefactor of human kind. In these characters, I have known him, and not less in the virtues and charms of social life, for a period of fifty years, during which there was not an interruption or diminution of mutual confidence and cordial friendship, for a single moment in a single instance. What I feel therefore now, need not, I should say, cannot, be expressed.

To Nicholas P. Trist, 6 July 1826
DLC: Trist Papers

Judicial Review

With respect to the supremacy of the Judicial power on questions occurring in the course of its functions, concerning the boundary of jurisdiction, between the United States and individual states, my opinion in favor of it was as the 41st No. of the Federalist shows, of the earliest date: and I have never ceased to think that this supremacy was a vital principle of the Constitution, as it is a prominent feature of its text. A supremacy of the Constitution and laws of the Union, without a supremacy in the exposition and execution of them, would be as much a mockery as a scabbard put into the hand of a soldier without a sword in it. I have never been able to see, that without such a view of the subject the Constitution itself could be the supreme law of the land; or that the *uniformity* of the Federal authority throughout the parties to it could be preserved; or that without this *unifor-mity*, anarchy and disunion could be prevented.

> To Nicholas P. Trist, December 1831
> DLC: Madison Papers

Justice

A wise nation will never permit those who relieve the wants of their Country, or who rely most on its faith, its firmness and its resources, when either of them is distrusted, to suffer by the event.

> Address to the States, 25 Apr. 1783
> *PJM* 6:493

Justice is the end of government. It is the end of civil society. It ever has been, and ever will be pursued, until it be obtained, or until liberty be lost in the pursuit.

> *The Federalist* No. 51, 6 Feb. 1788
> *PJM* 10:479

Knowledge

A popular Government, without popular information, or the means of acquiring it, is but a prologue to a Farce or a Tragedy; or perhaps both. Knowledge will forever govern ignorance: And a people who mean to be their own Governors, must arm themselves with the power which Knowledge gives.

> To William T. Barry, 4 Aug. 1822
> DLC: Madison Papers

Labor

There is one indelible cause remaining, of pressure on the condition of the laboring part of mankind: and that is, the constant tendency to an increase of their number, after the increase of food has reached its term. The competition for employment then reduces wages to their minimum, and privation to its maximum: and whether the evil proceeding from this tendency be checked, as it must be, by either physical or moral causes, the checks are themselves but so many evils. With this knowledge of the impossibility of banishing evil altogether from human society, we must console ourselves with the belief that it is overbalanced by the good mixed with it, and direct our efforts to an increase of the good proportion of the mixture.

To Nicholas P. Trist, April 1827
DLC: Trist Papers

Language

The use of words is to express ideas. Perspicuity therefore requires not only that the ideas should be distinctly formed, but that they should be expressed by words distinctly and exclusively appropriated to them. But no language is so copious as to supply words and phrases for every complex idea, or so correct as not to include many equivocally denoting different ideas. Hence it must happen, that however accurately objects may be discriminated in themselves, and however accurately the discrimination may be considered, the definition of them may be rendered inaccurate by the inaccuracy of the terms in which it is delivered. And this unavoidable inaccuracy must be greater or less, according to the complexity and novelty of the objects defined. When the Almighty himself condescends to address mankind in their own language, his meaning luminous as it must be, is rendered dim and doubtful, by the cloudy medium through which it is communicated.

The Federalist No. 37, 11 Jan. 1788
PJM 10:361–63

To provide for the purity, the uniformity, and the stability of language, is of great importance under many aspects; and especially as an encouragement to genius and to literary labours by extending the prospect of just rewards. A universal and immortal language is among the wishes never likely to be gratified: But all languages are more or less susceptible of improvement and of preservation; and none can be better entitled to the means of perfecting and fixing it, than that common to this Country and Great Britain, since there is none that seems destined for a greater and freer portion of the human family.

To William S. Cardell, March 1820
DLC: Madison Papers

All languages, written as well as oral, tho much less than oral, are liable to changes from causes, some of them inseparable from the nature of man, and the progress of society. A perfect remedy for the evil must therefore be unattainable. But as far as it may be attainable, the attempt is laudable; and next to compleat success is that of recording with admitted fidelity the state of a language at the epoch of the Record. In the exposition of laws, and even of Constitutions, how many important errors, may be produced by mere innovations in the use of words and phrases, if not controllable by a recurrence to the original, and authentic meaning attached to them.

To Sherman Converse, 10 Mar. 1826
DLC: Madison Papers

But the greatest difficulty as in every use of a foreign language, is in selecting the appropriate word or phrase among those differing in the shades of meaning, and where the meaning may be essentially varied by the particular application of them. Hence the mistakes sometimes ludicrous in the use of a foreign language, imperfectly understood; as in the case of the Frenchman, who finding in the Dictionary that to pickle meant to preserve, took leave of his friends with a God pickle you.

To Buckner Thruston, 1 Mar. 1833
DLC: Madison Papers

Law of Nations

A nation which appeals to law, rather [than] to force, is particularly bound to understand the use of the instrument [a treatise on international law] by which it wishes to maintain its rights, as well as of those which, against its wishes, it may be called on to employ. Where the Sword alone is the law, there is less inconsistency, if not more propriety in neglecting those Teachers of right and duty.

To Peter S. DuPonceau, 8 Dec. 1810
PJM-PS 3:60

Laws

Attempts to enforce by legal sanctions, acts obnoxious to so great a proportion of Citizens, tend to enervate the laws in general, and to slacken the bands of Society. If it be difficult to execute any law which is not generally deemed necessary or salutary, what must be the case, where it is deemed invalid and dangerous? And what may be the effect of so striking an example of impotency in the Government, on its general authority?

Memorial and Remonstrance,
20 June 1785
PJM 8:303

Lawyers

It [law] alone can bring into use many parts of knowledge you have acquired and will still have a taste for, and pay you for cultivating the Arts of Eloquence. It is a sort of General Lover that wooes all the Muses and Graces. . . . I greatly commend your determined adherence to probity and Truth in the Character of a Lawyer but fear it would be impracticable.

To William Bradford, 25 Sept. 1773
PJM 1:96

A Delicate Taste and warm imagination like yours must find it hard to give up such refined and exquisite enjoyments for the coarse and dry study of the Law: It is like leaving a pleasant flourishing field for a barren desert; perhaps I should not say barren either because the Law does bear fruit but it is sour fruit that must be gathered and pressed and distilled before it can bring pleasure or profit.

To William Bradford, 24 Jan. 1774
PJM 1:105

Leadership

The aim of every political constitution is, or ought to be, first, to obtain for rulers men who possess most wisdom to discern, and most virtue to pursue the common good of the society; and in the next place, to take the most effectual precautions for keeping them virtuous, whilst they continue to hold their public trust.

The Federalist No. 57, 19 Feb. 1788
PJM 10:521

Legislation

It will be of little avail to the people that the laws are made by men of their own choice, if the laws be so voluminous that they cannot be read, or so incoherent that they cannot be understood; if they be repealed or revised before they are promulged, or undergo such incessant changes that no man who knows what the law is today can guess what it will be to-morrow.

The Federalist No. 62, 27 Feb. 1788
PJM 10:539

Another effect of public instability is the unreasonable advantage it gives to the sagacious, the enterprising and the moneyed few, over the industrious and uninformed mass of the people. Every new regulation concerning commerce or revenue; or in any manner affecting the value of the different species of property, presents a new harvest to those who watch the change and can trace its consequences; a harvest reared not by themselves but by the toils and cares of the great body of their fellow citizens. This is a state of things in which it may be said with some truth that laws are made for the *few* not for the *many*.

The Federalist No. 62, 27 Feb. 1788
PJM 10:539–40

The greatest calamity to which the United States can be subject, is a vicissitude of laws, and continual shifting and changing from one object to another, which must expose the people to various inconveniences. This has a certain effect, of which sagacious men always have, and always will make an advantage. From whom is advantage made? From the industrious farmers and tradesmen, who are ignorant of the means of making such advantages.

> Speech in the Virginia Ratifying
> Convention, 11 June 1788
> *PJM* 11:118

As in laws, so in Constitutions, the best keys for the interpreter are the evils which they were meant to remedy, and the wants which they were required to supply.

> To Edward Everett, 14 Nov. 1831
> MHi

Legislative Power

In a government, where numerous and extensive prerogatives are placed in the hands of a hereditary monarch, the executive department is very justly regarded as the source of danger, and watched with all the jealousy which a zeal for liberty ought to inspire. In a democracy, where a multitude of people exercise in person the legislative functions, and are continually exposed by their incapacity for regular deliberation and concerted measures, to the ambitious intrigues of their executive magistrates, tyranny may well be apprehended on some favourable emergency, to start up in the same quarter. But in a representative republic, where the executive magistracy is carefully limited both in the extent and the duration of its power; and where the legislative power is exercised by an assembly, which is inspired by a supposed influence over the people with an intrepid confidence in its own strength; which is sufficiently numerous to feel all the passions which actuate a multitude; yet not so numerous as to be incapable of pursuing the objects of its passions, by means which reason prescribes; it is against the enterprising am-

bition of this department, that the people ought to indulge all
their jealousy and exhaust all their precautions.

> The Federalist No. 48, 1 Feb. 1788
> PJM 10:457

One of the best securities against the creation of unnecessary
offices or tyrannical powers, is an exclusion of the authors from
all share in filling the one, or influence in the execution of the
others.

> Observations on Jefferson's Draft
> Constitution, 15 Oct. 1788
> PJM 11:289

Legislators

Representative appointments are sought from 3 motives. 1. ambition 2. personal interest. 3. public good. Unhappily the two
first are proved by experience to be most prevalent. Hence the
candidates who feel them, particularly, the second, are most industrious, and most successful in pursuing their object: and
forming often a majority in the legislative Councils, with interested views, contrary to the interest, and views, of their Constituents, join in a perfidious sacrifice of the latter to the former.
A succeeding election it might be supposed, would displace the
offenders, and repair the mischief. But how easily are base and
selfish measures, masked by pretexts of public good and apparent expediency? How frequently will a repetition of the same
arts and industry which succeeded in the first instance, again
prevail on the unwary to misplace their confidence? How frequently too will the honest but unenlightened representative be
the dupe of a favorite leader, veiling his selfish views under the
professions of public good, and varnishing his sophistical arguments with the glowing colours of popular eloquence?

> "Vices of the Political System,"
> April 1787
> PJM 9:354

Legislatures

The truth is, that in all cases a certain number [of legislators] at least seems to be necessary to secure the benefits of free consultation and discussion, and to guard against too easy a combination for improper purposes: As on the other hand, the number ought at most to be kept within a certain limit, in order to avoid the confusion and intemperance of a multitude. In all very numerous assemblies, of whatever characters composed, passion never fails to wrest the sceptre from reason. Had every Athenian citizen been a Socrates, every Athenian assembly would still have been a mob.

The Federalist No. 55, 13 Feb. 1788
PJM 10:505

Liberty

If justice, good faith, honor, gratitude and all the other Qualities which enoble the character of a nation, and fulfil the ends of Government, be the fruits of our establishments, the cause of liberty will acquire a dignity and lustre, which it has never yet enjoyed; and an example will be set which can not but have the most favorable influence on the rights of mankind.

Address to the States, 25 Apr. 1783
PJM 6:494

In bestowing the eulogies due to the partitions and internal checks of power, it ought not the less to be remembered, that they are neither the sole nor the chief palladium of constitutional liberty. The people who are the authors of this blessing, must also be its guardians. Their eyes must be ever ready to mark, their voice to pronounce, and their arm to repel or repair aggressions on the authority of their constitutions; the highest authority next to their own, because the immediate work of their own, and the most sacred part of their property, as recognising and recording the title to every other.

National Gazette essay, 4 Feb. 1792
PJM 14:218

Who are the Best Keepers of the People's Liberties? The people themselves. The sacred trust can be no where so safe as in the hands most interested in preserving it. . . . Although all men are born free, and all nations might be so, yet too true it is, that slavery has been the general lot of the human race. Ignorant— they have been cheated; asleep—they have been surprized; divided—the yoke has been forced upon them. But what is the lesson? That because the people *may* betray themselves, they ought to give themselves up, blindfold, to those who have an interest in betraying them? Rather conclude that the people ought to be enlightened, to be awakened, to be united, that after establishing a government they should watch over it, as well as obey it.

National Gazette essay, 20 Dec. 1792
PJM 14:426

Liberty disdains to persecute.

National Gazette essay, 20 Dec. 1792
PJM 14:427

Libraries

A tree of useful knowledge planted in every neighbourhood, would help to make a paradise, as that of forbidden use occasioned the loss of one.

To Jesse Torrey, Jr., 30 Jan. 1822
DLC: Madison Papers

Dolley Payne Madison

I received some days ago your precious favor from Fredricksburg. I can not express, but hope you will conceive the joy it gave me: The delay in hearing of your leaving Hanover which I regarded as the only satisfactory proof of your recovery, had filled me with extreme disquietude, and the communication of the welcome event was endeared to me by the *style* in which it was conveyed. I hope you will never have another *deliberation*, on that subject. If the sentiments of my heart can guarantee those of yours, they assure me there can never be a cause for it.

> To Dolley Payne Todd, 18 Aug. 1794
> *PJM* 15:351

Your second letter my dearest of the 26. continued on the 28. is this moment received; and flatters my anxious wishes and hopes for your perfect recovery, and your *safe* return to Washington. I am glad to find you so determined in your adherence to the Doctor's prescriptions. . . . I repeat my kisses to Miss P[Betsy Pemberton]. I wish I could give her more substantial ones than can be put on paper. She shall know the difference between them the moment she presents her sweet lips in Washington—after I have set the example on those of another person whose name I flatter myself you will not find it difficult to guess. I shall comply with all the commands in your letter. With unalterable love I remain Yrs.

> To Dolley Payne Madison, 31 Oct. 1805
> NjP

I wrote you my beloved by the mail of Tuesday, and hoped it would be the last from this place [Charlottesville], with fears however that overbalanced hope. It appears now not to be certain that I shall be able to get away even tomorrow. Every exertion however will be made to effect it. . . . I can not express my anxiety to be with you; I hope never again to be so long from you, being with devoted affection ever yours.

> To Dolley Payne Madison, 14 Dec. 1826
> PCarlD

Majority Rule

There is no maxim in my opinion which is more liable to be misapplied, and which therefore more needs elucidation than the current one that the interest of the majority is the political standard of right and wrong. Taking the word "interest" as synonymous with "Ultimate happiness," in which sense it is qualified with every necessary moral ingredient, the proposition is no doubt true. But taking it in the popular sense, as referring to immediate augmentation of property and wealth, nothing can be more false. In the latter sense it would be the interest of the majority in every community to despoil and 'enslave the minority of individuals; and in a federal community to make a similar sacrifice of the minority of the component States. In fact it is only reestablishing under another name and a more specious form, force as the measure of right.

To James Monroe, 5 Oct. 1786
PJM 9:141

All civilized societies are divided into different interests and factions, as they happen to be creditors or debtors—Rich or poor—husbandmen, merchants or manufacturers—members of different religious sects—followers of different political leaders—inhabitants of different districts—owners of different kinds of property &c &c. In republican Government the majority however composed, ultimately give the law. Whenever therefore an apparent interest or common passion unites a majority what is to restrain them from unjust violations of the rights and interests of the minority, or of individuals? Three motives only 1. a prudent regard to their own good as involved in the general and permanent good of the Community. This consideration although of decisive weight in itself, is found by experience to be too often unheeded. It is too often forgotten, by nations as well as by individuals that honesty is the best policy. 2dly. respect for character. However strong this motive may be in individuals, it is considered as very insufficient to restrain them from injustice.

In a multitude its efficacy is diminished in proportion to the number which is to share the praise or the blame. Besides, as it has reference to public opinion, which within a particular Society, is the opinion of the majority, the standard is fixed by those whose conduct is to be measured by it. . . . 3dly. will Religion the only remaining motive be a sufficient restraint? It is not pretended to be such on men individually considered. Will its effect be greater on them considered in an aggregate view? quite the reverse. The conduct of every popular assembly acting on oath, the strongest of religious Ties, proves that individuals join without remorse in acts, against which their consciences would revolt if proposed to them under the like sanction, separately in their closets.

"Vices of the Political System,"
April 1787
PJM 9:355–56

Wherever the real power in a Government lies, there is the danger of oppression. In our Governments the real power lies in the majority of the Community, and the invasion of private rights is *chiefly* to be apprehended, not from acts of Government contrary to the sense of its constituents, but from acts in which the Government is the mere instrument of the major number of the constituents. . . . Wherever there is an interest and power to do wrong, wrong will generally be done, and not less readily by a powerful and interested party than by a powerful and interested prince.

To Thomas Jefferson, 17 Oct. 1788
PJM 11:298

Militia

Always remembering, that an Armed and trained militia is the firmest bulwark of Republics; that without standing Armies their liberty can never be in danger; nor with large ones, safe.

First Inaugural Address, 4 Mar. 1809
PJM-PS 1:17

Mississippi River

The use of the Mississippi is given by Nature to our Western Country, and no power on Earth can take it from them. Whilst we assert our title to it therefore with a becoming firmness let us not forget that we can not ultimately be deprived of it, and that for the present, war is more than all things to be deprecated.

To James Monroe, 8 Jan. 1785
PJM 8:220

Monopolies

Perpetual monopolies of every sort, are forbidden not only by the genius of free Governments, but by the imperfection of human foresight.

Detached Memoranda, *post* 1817
DLC: Rives Collection, Madison Papers

James Monroe

The effect of this [sale of Monroe's Virginia estate], in closing the prospect of our ever meeting again afflicts me deeply, certainly not less so than it can you. The pain I feel at the idea, associated as it is with a recollection of the long, close and uninterrupted friendship which united us, amounts to a pang which I cannot well express, and which makes me seek for an alleviation in the possibility that you may be brought back to us in the wonted degree of intercourse.

To James Monroe, 21 Apr. 1831
DLC: Monroe Papers

I need not say to you who so well know, how highly I rated the comprehensiveness and character of his mind; the purity and nobleness of his principles; the importance of his patriotic services; and the many private virtues of which his whole life was a model, nor how deeply therefore I must sympathize, on his loss, with those who feel it most. A close friendship, continued thro' so long a period and such diversified scenes, had grown into an affection very imperfectly expressed by that term; and I value accordingly the manifestation in his last hours that the reciprocity never abated.

> To Tench Ringgold, 12 July 1831
> DLC: Madison Papers

Morality

He [Madison] had been animadverted upon, for appealing to the heart as well as the head: he would be bold, nevertheless, to repeat, that, in great and unusual questions of morality, the heart is the best casuist.

> Speech in Congress, 18 Feb. 1790
> *PJM* 13:49

Naturalization

When we are considering the advantages that may result from an easy mode of naturalization, we ought also to consider the cautions necessary to guard against abuses; it is no doubt very desirable, that we should hold out as many inducements as possible, for the worthy part of mankind to come and settle amongst us, and throw their fortunes into a common lot with ours. But, why is this desirable? Not merely to swell the catalogue of people. No, sir, 'tis to encrease the wealth and strength of the community, and those who acquire the rights of citizenship, without adding to the strength or wealth of the community, are not the people we are in want of. . . . I should be exceedingly sorry, sir, that our rule of naturalization excluded a single person of good fame, that really meant to incorporate himself into our society; on the other hand, I do not wish that any man should acquire the privilege, but who, in fact, is a real addition to the wealth or strength of the United States.

> Speech in Congress, 3 Feb. 1790
> *PJM* 13:17

Old Age

In explanation of my microscopic writing, I must remark that the older I grow, the more my stiffening fingers make smaller letters, as my feet take shorter steps; the progress in both cases being at the same time more fatiguing as well as more slow.

To James Monroe, 21 Apr. 1831
DLC: Monroe Papers

Having outlived so many of my co-temporaries I ought not to forget that I may be thought to have outlived myself.

To Jared Sparks, 1 June 1831
DLC: Madison Papers

Doctor Dunglison being with us and in the habit of drinking Sherry, and a better judge than I could be were my palate in better health, pronounces the wine to be of the first chop. It is I doubt not very fine, and I wish I could more safely indulge a relish for it. It gives me pleasure to learn that you can safely do so, and I hope the Sherry may prove with you what has been said of good wine, a milk for old age.

To James Maury, 26 May 1836
DLC: Madison Papers

Original Intent

But, after all, whatever veneration might be entertained for the body of men who formed our constitution, the sense of that body could never be regarded as the oracular guide in the expounding the constitution. As the instrument came from them, it was nothing more than the draught of a plan, nothing but a dead letter, until life and validity were breathed into it, by the voice of the people, speaking through the several state conventions. If we were to look therefore, for the meaning of the instrument, beyond the face of the instrument, we must look for it not in the general convention, which proposed, but in the state conventions, which accepted and ratified the constitution.

Speech in Congress, 6 Apr. 1796
PJM 16:295–96

As a guide in expounding and applying the provisions of the Constitution, the debates and incidental decisions of the Convention can have no authoritative character. . . . The legitimate meaning of the Instrument must be derived from the text itself; or if a key is to be sought elsewhere, it must be not in the opinions or intentions of the Body which planned and proposed the Constitution, but in the sense attached to it by the people in their respective State Conventions where it received all the authority which it possesses.

To Thomas Ritchie, 15 Sept. 1821
DLC: Madison Papers

But whatever might have been the opinions entertained in forming the Constitution, it was the duty of all to support it in its true meaning as understood *by the Nation* at the time of its ratification.

To John G. Jackson, 28 Dec. 1821
DLC: Madison Papers

If the instrument [the U.S. Constitution] be interpreted by criticisms which lose sight of the intention of the parties to it, in the fascinating pursuit of objects of public advantage or convenience, the purest motives can be no security against innovations materially changing the features of the Government.

To Andrew Stevenson, 25 Mar. 1826
DLC: Madison Papers

Paper Money

Whether Virginia is to remain exempt from the epidemic malady [paper currency] will depend on the ensuing Assembly. My hopes rest chiefly on the exertions of Col. Mason and the failure of the experiments elsewhere. That these must fail is morally certain; for besides the proofs of it already visible in some States, and the intrinsic defect of the paper in all, this fictitious money will rather feed than cure the spirit of extravagance which sends away the coin to pay the unfavorable balance, and will therefore soon be carried to market to buy up coin for that purpose. From that moment depreciation is inevitable. The value of money consists in the uses it will serve. Specie will serve all the uses of paper. Paper will not serve one of the essential uses of specie. The paper therefore will be less valuable than specie.

To Thomas Jefferson, 12 Aug. 1786
PJM 9:95

Peace

A universal and perpetual peace, it is to be feared, is in the catalogue of events, which will never exist but in the imaginations of visionary philosophers, or in the breasts of benevolent enthusiasts. It is still however true, that war contains so much folly, as well as wickedness, that much is to be hoped from the progress of reason; and if any thing is to be hoped, every thing ought to be tried.

National Gazette essay, 31 Jan. 1792
PJM 14:207

Political Harassment

By what rule then, or upon what principle, shall a man be rewarded or punished, for the fair exercise of his judgment, especially when called on to give it, by obligations he could not resist, and upon a point, in which in preference to all others, the most unbounded freedom should be used? I had supposed that if his decision was a wise one, the benefits of the system were to be his compensation; if he erred, his own and the calamities of his country, the punishment; that the question involved in it, neither in the origin, nor its consequences, considerations of a personal nature, and that of course the conduct of no man, in relation to this object, be it what it might, merited reward or punishment. I could wish that those political casuists, who are acquainted with the transactions on the great theatre, would solve this problem; for to me it seems indispensibly necessary that those who arraign a fellow citizen, before the bar of the public, should at least demonstrate that a charge with which he is accused, contains in it something criminal.

> *Dunlap's American Daily Advertiser* essay,
> 22 Sept. 1792
> *PJM* 14:369

Intemperance in politics is bad enough. Intolerance has no excuse.

> To Joseph C. Cabell, 18 Mar. 1827
> DLC: Madison Papers

Political Management

This picture of our affairs [in the summer of 1783] is not a flattering one; but we have been witnesses of so many cases in which evils and errors have been the parents of their own remedy, that we can not but view it with the consolations of hope.

> To Thomas Jefferson, 11 Aug. 1783
> *PJM* 7:269

The war if it takes place will be made to solve many things, so as to take credit from the public measures. Candid people however will be sensible that the greater part of political management consists rather in taking advantage of events as they occur, than in precisely forseeing or inviting them.

> To Isaac Hite, 22 June 1803
> *Charles Hamilton Catalogue* 119,
> April 1979

Political Parties

The existing tranquility and harmony on the public feeling the result of the propitious evanescence of the causes of discord is a just subject of congratulation. It is to be wished that they may never be interrupted by the worst of all political divisions; one founded on Geographical boundaries and embittered by another descrimination among the States which happens to coincide with them. Political parties intermingled throughout the community unite as well as divide every Section of it. Parties founded on local distinctions and fixed peculiarities which Separate the whole into great conflicting masses are far more to be dreaded in their tendency.

To Richard Bland Lee, 5 Aug. 1819
DLC: Madison Papers

There seems to be a propensity in free Governments which will always find or make subjects, on which human opinions and passions may be thrown into conflict. The most perhaps that can be counted on and that will be sufficient is that occasions for party contests in such a Country and Government as ours, will be either so slight or so transient, as not to threaten any permanent or dangerous consequences to the character and prosperity of the Republic.

To James Monroe, 18 May 1822
DLC: Madison Papers

Besides the occasional and transient subjects on which parties are formed, they seem to have a permanent foundation in the variance of political opinions in free States, and of occupations and interests in all civilized States. The Constitution itself, whether written or prescriptive, influenced as its exposition and administration will be, by those causes, must be an unfailing source of party distinctions. And the very peculiarity which gives pre-eminent value to that of the United States, the partition of power between different governments, as well as between different departments of Government, opens a new door for controversies and parties. There is nevertheless sufficient scope for combating the spirit of party, as far as it may not be necessary to fan the flame of liberty, in efforts to divert it from the more noxious channels; to moderate its violence, especially in the ascendant party; to elucidate the policy which harmonizes jealous interests; and particularly to give to the Constitution that just construction, which with the aid of time and habit, may put an end to the more dangerous schisms otherwise growing out of it.

To Henry Lee, 25 June 1824
DLC: Madison Papers

Political Popularity

I trust it is equally impossible for the result [of the election] whatever it may be, to rob me of any reflections which enter into the internal fund of comfort and happiness. Popular favor or disfavor, is no criterion of the character maintained with those whose esteem an honorable ambition must court. Much less can it be a criterion of that maintained with ones self. And when the spirit of party directs the public voice, it must be a little mind indeed that can suffer in its own estimation, or apprehend danger of suffering in that of others.

To Edmund Randolph, 2 Nov. 1788
PJM 11:329–30

Politics

Political Contests are necessary sometimes as well as military to afford exercise and practise and to instruct in the Art of defending Liberty and property.

To William Bradford, 24 Jan. 1774
PJM 1:105

Nothing is more common here, and I presume the case must be the same with you, than to see companies of intelligent people equally divided, and equally earnest [on the question of adopting the U.S. Constitution], in maintaining on one side that the General Government will overwhelm the State Governments, and on the other that it will be a prey to their encroachments; on the one side that the structure of the Government is too firm and too strong, and on the other that it partakes too much of the weakness and instability of the Governments of the particular

States. What is the proper conclusion from all this? That unanimity is not to be expected in any great political question: that the danger is probably exaggerated on each side, when an opposite danger is conceived on the opposite side—that if any Constitution is to be established by deliberation and choice, it must be examined with many allowances, and must be compared not with the theory, which each individual may frame in his own mind, but with the system which it is meant to take the place of, and with any other which there might be a probability of obtaining.

To Archibald Stuart, 30 Oct. 1787
PJM 10:232

It is a misfortune, inseparable from human affairs, that public measures are rarely investigated with that spirit of moderation which is essential to a just estimate of their real tendency to advance or obstruct the public good; and that this spirit is more apt to be diminished than promoted, by those occasions which require an unusual exercise of it.

The Federalist No. 37, 11 Jan. 1788
PJM 10:359

Population

I have no doubt that the misery of the lower classes will be found to abate wherever the Government assumes a freer aspect, and the laws favor a subdivision of property. Yet I suspect that the difference will not fully account for the comparative comfort of the Mass of people in the United States. Our limited population has probably as large a share in producing this effect as the political advantages which distinguish us. A certain degree of misery seems inseparable from a high degree of populousness. . . . No problem in political œconomy has appeared to me more puzzling than that which relates to the most proper distribution of the inhabitants of a Country fully peopled.

To Thomas Jefferson, 19 June 1786
PJM 9:76

Poverty and Government

To provide employment for the poor and support for the indigent is among the primary, and at the same time not least difficult cares of the public authority. In very populous Countries the task is particularly arduous. In our favored Country where employment and food are much less subject to failures or deficiencies the interposition of the public guardianship is required in a far more limited degree. Some degree of interposition nevertheless, is at all times and every where called for.

> To Frederick C. Schaeffer, 8 Jan. 1820
> DLC: Madison Papers

Power

All men having power ought to be distrusted to a certain degree.

> Speech in the Constitutional
> Convention, 11 July 1787
> *PJM* 10:98

It cannot have escaped those who have attended with candour to the arguments employed against the extensive powers of the government, that the authors of them have very little considered how far these powers were necessary means of attaining a necessary end. They have chosen rather to dwell on the inconveniences which must be unavoidably blended with all political advantages; and on the possible abuses which must be incident to every power or trust of which a beneficial use can be made. This method of handling the subject cannot impose on the good sense of the people of America. It may display the subtlety of the writer; it may open a boundless field for rhetoric and declamation; it may inflame the passions of the unthinking, and may confirm the prejudices of the misthinking. But cool and candid people will at once reflect, that the purest of human blessings must have a portion of alloy in them; that the choice must always be made, if not of the lesser evil, at least of the GREATER, not the PERFECT good; and that in every political institution, a power to advance the public happiness involves a discretion which may be misapplied and abused. They will see therefore that in all cases, where power is to be conferred, the point first to be decided is whether such a power be necessary to the public good; as the next will be, in case of an affirmative decision, to guard as effectually as possible against a perversion of the power to the public detriment.

The Federalist No. 41, 19 Jan. 1788
PJM 10:391

All power in human hands is liable to be abused. In Governments independent of the people, the rights and interests of the whole may be sacrificed to the views of the Government. In Republics, where the people govern themselves, and where of course the majority govern, a danger to the minority, arises from opportunities tempting a sacrifice of their rights to the interests real or supposed of the Majority. No form of Government therefore can be a perfect guard against the abuse of power. The recommendation of the Republican form is that the danger of abuse is less than in any other and the superior recommendation of the federo-Republican system is, that, whilst it provides more effectually against external danger, it involves a greater security to the minority against the hasty formation of oppressive majorities.

To Thomas Ritchie, 18 Dec. 1825
DLC: Madison Papers

Power of the Purse

This power over the purse, may in fact be regarded as the most compleat and effectual weapon with which any constitution can arm the immediate representatives of the people, for obtaining a redress of every grievance, and for carrying into effect every just and salutary measure.

The Federalist No. 58, 20 Feb. 1788
PJM 10:530

Precedent

On the subject of the Bank [of the United States] alone is there a color for the charge of mutability [on Madison's part] on a Constitutional question. But here the inconsistency is apparent, not real, since the change was in conformity to an early and un-changed opinion, that in the case of a Constitution as of a law a course of authoritative, deliberate and continued decisions, such as the Bank could plead, was an evidence of the public judgment, necessarily superseding individual opinions.

To Nicholas P. Trist, December 1831
DLC: Madison Papers

Former Presidents and Politics

An active zeal in those who have been honored with the trust most exposed to public jealousy, in designating and procuring Successors, is not only unbecoming, but on that very account, forfeits the influence at which it aims. Nor should it be forgot-ten, that after passing the canonical age of three score and ten, few individual characters can escape successful allusions to the presumptive operation of time in dimming the intellectual vi-sion as well as the corporeal.

To Jonathan Roberts, 29 Feb. 1828
DLC: Madison Papers

The Press

And to that of the press [as an occupation] in particular, what well-founded objection can be opposed? Is it less honorable, less beneficial to mankind than all others? and does the American [Alexander Hamilton] come forward to traduce and lessen it in the estimation of the public? Vain and unworthy effort! For whilst its services shall be remembered in raising man from a low and degraded state of barbarism to the high improvement of his talents, in the perfection of the arts and sciences, which forms the proud boast of modern times, every attempt of this kind must be reprobated.

Dunlap's American Daily Advertiser essay,
20 Oct. 1792
PJM 14:390

Some degree of abuse is inseparable from the proper use of every thing; and in no instance is this more true, than in that of the press. It has accordingly been decided by the practice of the states, that it is better to leave a few of its noxious branches, to their luxuriant growth, than by pruning them away, to injure the vigor of those yielding the proper fruits. And can the wisdom of this policy be doubted by any who reflect, that to the press alone, chequered as it is with abuses, the world is indebted for all the triumphs which have been gained by reason and humanity, over error and oppression; who reflect that to the same beneficent source, the United States owe much of the lights which conducted them to the rank of a free and independent nation; and which have improved their political system, into a shape so auspicious to their happiness.

The Report of 1800, 7 Jan. 1800
PJM 17:338

There is but too much truth in the picture of newspapers as sketched in the letter to the Philadelphia printer. But the effect of their falsehood and slanders, must always be controlled in a certain degree by contradictions in rival or hostile papers, where the press is free. The complaint nevertheless applies with much force to the one sided publications which may happen to predominate at particular periods, or under particular circumstances. It is then that the minds best disposed, may be filled with the most gross and injurious untruths. Those who see erroneous statements of facts without ever seeing a contradiction of them, and specious comments without any exposure of their fallacies, will of course be generally under the delusions so strongly painted by Mr. Jefferson. It has been said, that any Country might be governed at the will of one, who had the exclusive privilege of furnishing its popular songs. The result would be far more certain from a monopoly of the politics of the press. Could it be so arranged, that every newspaper when printed on one side should be handed over to the press of an adversary, to be printed on the other; thus presenting to every reader both sides of every question, truth would always have a fair chance.

To Nicholas P. Trist, 23 Apr. 1828
DLC: Trist Papers

Property

If *all* power be suffered to slide into hands not interested in the rights of property which must be the case whenever a majority fall under that description, one of two things cannot fail to happen; either they will unite against the other description and become the dupes and instruments of ambition, or their poverty and independence will render them the mercenary instruments of wealth. In either case liberty will be subverted; in the first by a despotism growing out of anarchy, in the second, by an oligarchy founded on corruption.

Observations on Jefferson's Draft
Constitution, 15 Oct. 1788
PJM 11:288

In its larger and juster meaning, it embraces every thing to which a man may attach a value and have a right; and *which leaves to every one else the like advantage.* In the former sense, a man's land, or merchandize, or money is called his property. In the latter sense, a man has a property in his opinions and the free communication of them. He has a property of peculiar value in his religious opinions, and in the profession and practice dictated by them. He has a property very dear to him in the safety and liberty of his person. He has an equal property in the free use of his faculties and free choice of the objects on which to employ them. In a word, as a man is said to have a right to his property, he may be equally said to have a property in his rights. Where an excess of power prevails, property of no sort is duly respected. No man is safe in his opinions, his person, his faculties, or his possessions. Where there is an excess of liberty, the effect is the same, tho' from an opposite cause. Government is instituted to protect property of every sort; as well that which lies in the various rights of individuals, as that which the term particularly expresses. This being the end of government, that alone is a *just* government, which *impartially* secures to every man, whatever is his *own*.

National Gazette essay, 27 Mar. 1792
PJM 14:266

Public Debt

I regret, as much as any member, the unavoidable weight and duration of the burdens [the Revolutionary War debt] to be imposed; having never been a proselyte to the doctrine, that public debts are public benefits. I consider them, on the contrary, as evils which ought to be removed as fast as honor and justice will permit, and shall heartily join in the means necessary for that purpose.

Speech in Congress, 11 Feb. 1790
PJM 13:38

I have received your reflections on the subject of a public debt with pleasure—in general they are in my opinion just and important. Perhaps it is not possible to shun some of the evils you point out, without abandoning too much the reestablishment of public credit. But as far as this object will permit I go on the principle that a Public Debt is a Public curse and in a Republican Government a greater than in any other.

To Henry Lee, 13 Apr. 1790
PJM 13:148

Public Good

We have heard of the impious doctrine in the old world that the people were made for kings, not kings for the people. Is the same doctrine to be revived in the new, in another shape, that the solid happiness of the people is to be sacrificed to the views of political institutions of a different form? It is too early for politicians to presume on our forgetting that the public good, the real welfare of the great body of the people is the supreme object to be pursued; and that no form of government whatever, has any other value, than as it may be fitted for the attainment of this object.

The Federalist No. 45, 26 Jan. 1788
PJM 10:428–29

Public Opinion

If we are to take for the criterion of truth the majority of suffrages, they ought to be gathered from those philosophical and patriotic citizens who cultivate their reason, apart from the scenes which distract its operations, and expose it to the influence of the passions. The advantage enjoyed by public bodies in the light struck out by the collision of arguments, is but too often overbalanced by the heat proceeding from the same source. Many other sources of involuntary error might be added. It is no reflection on Congress to admit for one, the united voice of the place, where they may happen to deliberate. Nothing is more contagious than opinion, especially on questions, which being susceptible of very different glosses, beget in the mind a distrust of itself. It is extremely difficult also to avoid confounding the local with the public opinion, and to withhold the respect due to the latter, from the fallacious specimens exhibited by the former.

To Benjamin Rush, 7 Mar. 1790
PJM 13:93–94

Public opinion sets bounds to every government, and is the real sovereign in every free one. As there are cases where the public opinion must be obeyed by the government; so there are cases, where not being fixed, it may be influenced by the government. This distinction, if kept in view, would prevent or decide many

debates on the respect due from the government to the sentiments of the people.

National Gazette essay, 19 Dec. 1791
PJM 14:170

The larger a country, the less easy for its real opinion to be as-
certained, and the less difficult to be counterfeited; when ascer-
tained or presumed, the more respectable it is in the eyes of
individuals. This is favorable to the authority of government.
For the same reason, the more extensive a country, the more in-
significant is each individual in his own eyes. This may be unfavorable to liberty.

National Gazette essay, 19 Dec. 1791
PJM 14:170

Opinions whose only root is in the passions, must wither as the
subsiding of these withdraws the necessary pabulum.

To Richard Rush, 17 Jan. 1829
DLC: Madison Papers

Public Servants

In no case ought the eyes of the people to be shut on the conduct
of those entrusted with power; nor their tongues tied from a just
wholesome censure on it, any more than from merited commen-
dations. If neither gratitude for the honor of the trust, nor responsibility for the use of it, be sufficient to curb the unruly
passions of public functionaries, add new bits to the bridle rather
than to take it off altogether. This is the precept of common
sense illustrated and enforced by experience—uncontrolled
power, ever has been, and ever will be administered by the passions more than by reason.

"Political Reflections," 23 Feb. 1799
PJM 17:239

Public Service

The same fidelity to the public interest which obliges those who
are its appointed guardians, to pursue with every vigor a perfid-

ious or dishonest servant of the public requires them to confront
the imputations of malice against the good and faithful one.

> To Edmund Randolph, 4 June 1782
> *PJM* 4:313

Religion and the State

Happily for the states, they enjoy the utmost freedom of religion. This freedom arises from that multiplicity of sects, which
pervades America, and which is the best and only security for
religious liberty in any society. For where there is such a variety
of sects, there cannot be a majority of any one sect to oppress
and persecute the rest. Fortunately for this commonwealth [Vir-
ginia], a majority of the people are decidedly against any exclusive establishment—I believe it to be so in the other states.
There is not a shadow of right in the general government to
intermeddle with religion. Its least interference with it would be
a most flagrant usurpation.

> Speech in the Virginia Ratifying
> Convention, 12 June 1788
> *PJM* 11:130

As to those employed in teaching and inculcating the duties of
religion, there may be some indelicacy in singling them out [as
a category in a census], as the general government is proscribed
from interfering, in any manner whatever, in matters respecting
religion; and it may be thought to do this, in ascertaining who,
and who are not, ministers of the gospel.

> Speech in Congress, 2 Feb. 1790
> *PJM* 13:16

Is the appointment of Chaplains to the two Houses of Congress
consistent with the Constitution, and with the pure principle of
religious freedom? In strictness the answer on both points must
be in the negative. The Constitution of the U.S. forbids every
thing like an establishment of a national religion. The law ap-
pointing Chaplains establishes a religious worship for the national representatives, to be performed by Ministers of religion,

elected by a majority of them; and these are to be paid out of the national taxes. Does not this involve the principle of a national establishment, applicable to a provision for a religious worship for the Constituent as well as of the representative Body, approved by the majority, and conducted by Ministers of religion paid by the entire nation. The establishment of the chaplainship to Congress is a palpable violation of equal rights, as well as of Constitutional principles. The tenets of the Chaplains elected shut the door of worship against the members whose creeds and consciences forbid a participation in that of the majority. To say nothing of other sects, this is the case with that of Roman Catholics and Quakers who have always had members in one or both of the Legislative branches. Could a Catholic clergyman ever hope to be appointed a Chaplain? To say that religious principles are obnoxious or that his sect is small, is to lift the veil at once and exhibit in its naked deformity the doctrine that religious truth is to be tested by numbers, or that the major sects have a right to govern the minor.

> Detached Memoranda, *post* 1817
> DLC: Rives Collection, Madison Papers

It was the universal opinion of the Century preceding the last, that civil Government could not stand without the prop of a religious establishment, and that the Christian religion itself, would perish if not supported by a legal provision for its Clergy. The experience of Virginia conspicuously corroborates the disproof of both opinions. The Civil Government tho' bereft of everything like an anointed hierarchy possesses the requisite Stability and performs its functions with complete success: Whilst the number, the industry, and the morality of the priesthood and the devotion of the people have been manifestly increased by the total separation of the Church from the State.

> To Robert Walsh, Jr., 2 Mar. 1819
> DLC: Madison Papers

The experience of the U.S. is a happy disproof of the error so long rooted in the unenlightened minds of well meaning Christians, as well as in the corrupt hearts of persecuting Usurpers, that without a legal incorporation of religious and civil polity, neither could be supported. A mutual independence is found most friendly to practical Religion, to social harmony, and to political prosperity.

To Frederick L. Schaeffer, 3 Dec. 1821
DLC: Madison Papers

Notwithstanding the general progress made within the two last centuries in favour of this branch of Liberty, and the full estab- lishment of it in some parts of our Country, there remains in others a strong bias toward the old error, that without some sort of alliance or coalition between Government and Religion nei- ther can be duly supported. Such indeed is the tendency to such a coalition, and such its corrupting influence on both the parties, that the danger can not be too guarded against and in a govern- ment of opinion, like ours, the only effectual guard, must be found in the soundness and Stability of the general opinion on the subject. Every new and successful example therefore of a perfect separation between ecclesiastical and Civil matters, is of importance, and I have no doubt that every new example will succeed, as every past one has done in showing that religion and Government will both exist in greater purity, the less they are mixed together.

To Edward Livingston, 10 July 1822
DLC: Madison Papers

The difficulty of reconciling the Christian mind to the absence of religious Tuition from a University, established by Law and at the common expense, is probably less with us [in Virginia] than with you [in Massachusetts]. The settled opinion here is that religion is essentially distinct from Civil Government and exempt from its cognizance; that a connection between them is injurious to both; that there are causes in the human breast, which ensure the perpetuity of religion without the aid of the law; that rival sects with equal rights, exercise mutual censor- ships in favor of good morals; that if new sects arise with absurd opinions or overheated imaginations, the proper remedies lie in time, forbearance, and example: that a legal establishment of Religion without a toleration, could not be thought of, and with a toleration, is no security for public quiet and harmony, but rather a source itself of discord and animosity: and, finally, that these opinions are supported by experience, which has shewn that every relaxation of the Alliance between Law and Religion, from the partial example of Holland, to its consummation in Pennsylvania, New Jersey &c. has been found as safe in practice as it is sound in Theory.

To Edward Everett, 19 Mar. 1823
DLC: Madison Papers

I must admit, moreover, that it may not be easy, in every possible case, to trace the line of separation, between the rights of Religion and the Civil authority, with such distinctions as to avoid collisions and doubts on unessential points. The tendency to a usurpation on one side, or the other, or to a corrupting coalition or alliance between them, will be best guarded against by an entire abstinance of the Government from interference, in any way whatever, beyond the necessity of preserving public order, and protecting each sect against trespasses on its legal rights by others.

To Jasper Adams, September 1833
MiU-C

Religious Establishments

Union of Religious Sentiments begets a surprizing confidence and Ecclesiastical Establishments tend to great ignorance and Corruption all of which facilitate the Execution of mischievous Projects.

To William Bradford, 24 Jan. 1774
PJM 1:105

It gives me much pleasure to observe by 2 printed reports sent me by Col. Grayson that in the latter Congress had expunged a clause contained in the first for setting apart a district of land in each Township, for supporting the Religion of the Majority of inhabitants. How a regulation, so unjust in itself, so foreign to the Authority of Congress so hurtful to the sale of the public land, and smelling so strongly of an antiquated Bigotry, could have received the countenance of a Committee is truly matter of astonishment.

To James Monroe, 29 May 1785
PJM 8:286

Who does not see that the same authority which can establish Christianity, in exclusion of all other Religions, may establish with the same ease any particular sect of Christians, in exclusion of all other Sects?

Memorial and Remonstrance,
20 June 1785
PJM 8:300

Torrents of blood have been spilt in the old world, by vain attempts of the secular arm, to extinguish Religious discord, by proscribing all difference in Religious opinion. Time has at length revealed the true remedy. Every relaxation of narrow and rigorous policy, wherever it has been tried, has been found to assuage the disease. The American Theatre has exhibited proofs that equal and compleat liberty, if it does not wholly eradicate it, sufficiently destroys its malignant influence on the health and prosperity of the State.

Memorial and Remonstrance,
20 June 1785
PJM 8:302-3

There may be less danger that Religion, if left to itself, will suffer from a failure of the pecuniary support applicable to it, than that an omission of the public authorities, to limit the duration of the charters to Religious corporations, and the amount of property acquirable by them, may lead to an injurious accumulation of wealth from the lavish donations and bequests prompted by a pious zeal or by an atoning remorse.

To Jasper Adams, September 1833
MiU-C

Religious Freedom

Religious bondage shackles and debilitates the mind and unfits it for every noble enterprize.

To William Bradford, 1 Apr. 1774
PJM 1:112–13

I have indeed as good an Atmosphere at home as the Climate will allow: but have nothing to brag of as to the State and Liberty of my Country. Poverty and Luxury prevail among all sorts: Pride ignorance and Knavery among the Priesthood and Vice and Wickedness among the Laity. This is bad enough But It is not the worst I have to tell you. That diabolical Hell conceived principle of persecution rages among some and to their eternal Infamy the Clergy can furnish their Quota of Imps for such business. This vexes me the most of any thing whatever. There are at this time in the adjacent County not less than 5 or 6 well meaning men in close Goal for publishing their religious Sentiments which in the main are very orthodox. I have neither patience to hear talk or think of any thing relative to this matter, for I have squabbled and scolded abused and ridiculed so long about it, to so little purpose that I am without common patience. So I leave you to pity me and pray for Liberty of Conscience to revive among us.

To William Bradford, 24 Jan. 1774
PJM 1:106

That religion, or the duty which we owe to our CREATOR, and the manner of discharging it, can be directed only by reason and conviction, not by force or violence; and therefore, all men are equally entitled to the free exercise of religion, according to the dictates of conscience; and that it is the mutual duty of all to practise Christian forbearance, love, and charity, towards each other.

Virginia Declaration of Rights,
12 June 1776
PJM 1:175

The preservation of a free Government requires not merely, that the metes and bounds which separate each department of power be invariably maintained; but more especially that neither of them be suffered to overleap the great Barrier which defends the rights of the people.

> Memorial and Remonstrance,
> 20 June 1785
> *PJM* 8:299

I have received your letter of the 6th. with the eloquent discourse delivered at the Consecration of the Jewish Synagogue. Having ever regarded the freedom of religious opinions and worship as equally belonging to every sect, and the secure enjoyment of it as the best human provision for bringing all either into the same way of thinking, or into that mutual charity which is the only proper substitute, I observe with pleasure the view you give of the spirit in which your Sect partake of the common blessings afforded by our Government and Laws.

> To Mordecai M. Noah, 15 May 1818
> DLC: Madison Papers

Among the features peculiar to the political system of the United States, is the perfect equality of rights which it secures to every religious sect. And it is particularly pleasing to observe in the good citizenship of such as have been most distrusted and oppressed elsewhere, a happy illustration of the safety and success of this experiment of a just and benignant policy. Equal laws protecting equal rights are found as they ought to be presumed, the best guarantee of loyalty and love of country; as well as best calculated to cherish that mutual respect and good will among Citizens of every religious denomination, which are necessary to social harmony and most favorable to the advancement of truth. The account you give of the Jews of your Congregation brings them fully within the scope of these observations.

> To Jacob de la Motta, August 1820
> DLC: Madison Papers

Ye States of America, which retain in your Constitutions or Codes, any aberration from the sacred principle of religious liberty, by giving to Caesar what belongs to God, or joining together what God has put asunder, hasten to revise and purify your systems, and make the example of your Country as pure and compleat, in what relates to the freedom of the mind and its allegiance to its maker, as in what belongs to the legitimate objects of political and civil institutions.

Detached Memoranda, *post* 1817
DLC: Rives Collection, Madison Papers

The danger of silent accumulations and encroachments by Ecclesiastical Bodies have not sufficiently engaged attention in the U.S. They have the noble merit of first unshackling the conscience from persecuting laws, and of establishing among religious Sects a legal equality. If some of the States have not embraced this just and this truly Christian principle in its proper latitude, all of them present examples by which the most enlightened States of the old world may be instructed; and there is one State at least, Virginia, where religious liberty is placed on its true foundation and is defined in its full latitude. The general principle is contained in her declaration of rights, prefixed to her Constitution: but it is unfolded and defined, in its precise extent, in the Act of the Legislature, usually named the Religious Bill, which passed into a law in the year 1786. Here the separation between the authority of human laws, and the natural rights of Man excepted from the grant on which all political authority is founded, is traced as distinctly as words can admit, and the limits to this authority established with as much solemnity as the forms of legislation can express. . . . This act is a true standard of Religious liberty: its principle the great barrier against usurpations on the rights of conscience. As long as it is respected and no longer, these will be safe. Every provision for them short of this principle, will be found to leave crevices at least, thro' which bigotry may introduce persecution; a monster, that feeding and thriving on its own venom, gradually swells to a size and strength overwhelming all laws divine and human.

Detached Memoranda, *post* 1817
DLC: Rives Collection, Madison Papers

Republicanism

He [Madison] conceived it to be a sound principle that an action innocent in the eye of the law, could not be the object of censure to a legislative body. When the people have formed a constitution, they retain those rights which they have not expressly delegated. It is a question whether what is thus retained can be legislated upon. Opinions are not the objects of legislation. . . . If we advert to the nature of republican government, we shall find that the censorial power is in the people over the government, and not in the government over the people.

Speech in Congress, 27 Nov. 1794
PJM 15:391

Republican Virtue

As there is a degree of depravity in mankind which requires a certain degree of circumspection and distrust: So there are other qualities in human nature, which justify a certain portion of esteem and confidence. Republican government presupposes the existence of these qualities in a higher degree than any other form. Were the pictures which have been drawn by the political jealousy of some among us, faithful likenesses of the human character, the inference would be that there is not sufficient virtue among men for self-government; and that nothing less than the chains of despotism can restrain them from destroying and devouring one another.

The Federalist No. 55, 13 Feb. 1788
PJM 10:507–8

Retirement

It is an error very naturally prevailing, that the retirement from public service, of which my case is an example, is a leisure for whatever pursuit might be most inviting. The truth however is, that I have rarely during the period of my public life, found my time less at my disposal than since I took my final leave of it.

> To Robert Walsh, Jr., 22 Dec. 1827
> DLC: Madison Papers

Right of Revolution

If there be a principle that ought not to be questioned within the United States, it is, that every nation has a right to abolish an old government and establish a new one. This principle is not only recorded in every public archive, written in every American heart, and sealed with the blood of a host of American martyrs; but is the only lawful tenure by which the United States hold their existence as a nation.

> *Helvidius* No. 3, 7 Sept. 1793
> *PJM* 15:98

Science

Experiment and comparison may be regarded as the two eyes of Philosophy, and it will require, I suspect, the best use of both, to reduce into a satisfactory system, the irregular and intermingled phenomena to be observed on the outside, and the penetrable inside of our little globe.

> To George W. Featherstonehaugh,
> 13 Mar. 1828
> DLC: Madison Papers

Secession

If South Carolina secedes it will be on the avowed grounds of her respect for the interposition of Virginia, and a reliance that

Virginia is to make a common cause with her throughout. In
that event and a continuance of the tariff laws, the prospect before us would be a rupture of the Union, a Southern Confed-
eracy, mutual enmity with the Northern, the most dreadful
animosities and border wars springing from the case of Slaves,
rival alliances abroad, standing armies at home to be supported
by internal taxes, and Federal Governments with powers of a
more consolidating and Monarchical tendency than the greatest
jealousy has charged on the existing system.

To Andrew Stevenson, 10 Feb. 1833
DLC: Madison Papers

The Senate

As the cool and deliberate sense of the community ought in all
governments, and actually will in all free governments ultimately prevail over the views of its rulers; so there are particular
moments in public affairs, when the people stimulated by some
irregular passion, or some illicit advantage, or misled by the art-
ful misrepresentations of interested men, may call for measures
which they themselves will afterwards be the most ready to la-
ment and condemn. In these critical moments, how salutary will
be the interference of some temperate and respectable body of
citizens, in order to check the misguided career, and to suspend
the blow meditated by the people against themselves, until reason, justice and truth, can regain their authority over the public mind?

The Federalist No. 63, 1 Mar. 1788
PJM 10:546

A Senate is to withstand the occasional impetuosities of the
more numerous branch. The members ought therefore to derive
a firmness from the tenure of their places. It ought to supply
the defect of knowledge and experience incident to the other
branch, there ought to be time given therefore for attaining the
qualifications necessary for that purpose. It ought finally to

maintain that system and steadiness in public affairs without which no Government can prosper or be respectable. This cannot be done by a body undergoing a frequent change of its members. A Senate for six years will not be dangerous to liberty. On the contrary it will be one of its best guardians. By correcting the infirmities of popular Government, it will prevent that disgust against that form which may otherwise produce a sudden transition to some very different one.

Observations on Jefferson's Draft
Constitution, 15 Oct. 1788
PJM 11:285–86

If the conduct and sentiments of the Senate on some occasions were to be regarded as the natural and permanent fruit of the institution, they ought to produce not only disgust but despair in all who are really attached to free Government.

To Thomas Jefferson, 4 Mar. 1798
PJM 17:89

Separation of Powers

Power being found by universal experience liable to abuses, a distribution of it into separate departments, has become a first principle of free governments. By this contrivance, the portion entrusted to the same hands being less, there is less room to abuse what is granted; and the different hands being interested, each in maintaining its own, there is less opportunity to usurp what is not granted. Hence the merited praise of governments modelled on a partition of their powers into legislative, executive, and judiciary, and a repartition of the legislative into different houses.

National Gazette essay, 4 Feb. 1792
PJM 14:217

Slavery

We have seen the mere distinction of colour made in the most enlightened period of time, a ground of the most oppressive dominion ever exercised by man over man.

> Speech at the Constitutional
> Convention, 6 June 1787
> *PJM* 10:33

In proportion as slavery prevails in a State, the Government, however democratic in name, must be aristocratic in fact. The power lies in a part instead of the whole; in the hands of property, not of numbers.

> Notes for Essays,
> 19 Dec. 1791–3 Mar. 1792
> *PJM* 14:163

The magnitude of this evil [slavery] among us is so deeply felt, and so universally acknowledged; that no merit could be greater than that of devising a satisfactory remedy for it.

> To Francis Wright, 1 Sept. 1825
> DLC: Madison Papers

Freedom of Speech

He [Madison] conceived it to be a sound principle that an action innocent in the eye of the law, could not be the object of censure to a legislative body. When the people have formed a constitution, they retain those rights which they have not expressly delegated. It is a question whether what is thus retained can be legislated upon. Opinions are not the objects of legislation. You animadvert on the *abuse* of reserved rights—how far will this go? It may extend to the liberty of speech and of the press.

> Speech in Congress, 27 Nov. 1794
> *PJM* 15:391

A Standing Army

A standing military force, with an overgrown Executive will not long be safe companions to liberty. The means of defence against foreign danger, have been always the instruments of tyranny at home. Among the Romans it was a standing maxim to excite a war, whenever a revolt was apprehended. Throughout all Europe, the armies kept up under the pretext of defending, have enslaved the people.

Speech at the Constitutional
Convention, 29 June 1787
PJM 10:87

Suffrage

The right of suffrage and the rule of apportionment are fundamentals in a free Government, and ought not to be submitted to Legislative discretion.

To Philip Doddridge, 6 June 1832
DLC: Madison Papers

Talent

In a Republic personal merit alone could be the ground of political exaltation, but it would rarely happen that this merit would be so pre-eminent as to produce universal acquiesence.

Speech in the Constitutional
Convention, 6 June 1787
PJM 10:35

Taxation

Taxes on consumption are always least burdensome, because they are least felt, and are borne too by those who are both willing and able to pay them; that of all taxes on consumption, those on foreign commerce are most compatible with the genius and policy of free States.

> Address to the States, 25 Apr. 1783
> *PJM* 6:489

[Mr. Madison] conceived taxes of all kinds to be evils in themselves, and that they were no otherwise admissible, than in order to avoid still greater evils. But of all the various kinds of taxes, he admitted the excise to be the most disagreeable; yet at the same time, he must say, that of the excise, that particular branch which related to ardent spirit was in itself the most proper; most likely to be productive, and least inconsistent with the spirit and disposition of the people of America.

> Speech in Congress, 6 Jan. 1791
> *PJM* 13:349

Term Limits

Experience constantly teaches that new members of a public body do not feel the necessary respect or responsibility for the acts of their predecessors, and that a change of members and *of circumstances* often proves fatal to consistency and stability of public measures.

> Notes on Debates, 6 Jan. 1783
> *PJM* 6:16

No man can be a competent legislator who does not add to an upright intention and a sound judgment, a certain degree of knowledge of the subjects on which he is to legislate. A part of this knowledge may be acquired by means of information which lie within the compass of men in private as well as public stations. Another part can only be attained, or at least thoroughly attained, by actual experience in the station which requires the use of it. The period of legislative service ought therefore in all such cases to bear some proportion to the extent of practical knowledge, requisite to the due performance of the service.

The Federalist No. 53, 9 Feb. 1788
PJM 10:490

A few of the members, as happens in all such assemblies, will possess superior talents; will, by frequent re-elections, become members of long standing; will be thoroughly masters of the public business, and perhaps not unwilling to avail themselves of those advantages. The greater proportion of new members, and the less the information of the bulk of the members, the more apt will they be to fall into the snares that may be laid for them.

The Federalist No. 53, 9 Feb. 1788
PJM 10:492

The ineligibility a second time [for an executive term], though not perhaps without advantages, is also liable to a variety of strong objections. It takes away one powerful motive to a faithful and useful administration, the desire of acquiring that title to a re-appointment. By rendering a periodical change of men necessary, it discourages beneficial undertakings which require perseverance and system, or, as frequently happened in the Roman Consulate, either precipitates or prevents the execution of them. It may inspire desperate enterprizes for the attainment of what is not attainable by legitimate means. It fetters the judgment and inclination of the Community; and in critical moments would either produce a violation of the Constitution, or exclude a choice which might be essential to the public safety. Add to the whole, that by putting the Executive Magistrate in the situation of the tenant of an unrenewable lease, it would tempt him to neglect the constitutional rights of his department, and to connive at usurpations by the Legislative department, with which he may connect his future ambition or interest.

Observations on Jefferson's Draft
Constitution, 15 Oct. 1788
PJM 11:289

Tobacco

I have received your favor of the 9th. with a copy of your Lecture on Tobacco and ardent spirits. It is a powerful dissuasion from the pernicious use of such stimulants. . . . . Its foreign translations and its reaching a fifth Edition are encouraging evidences of its usefulness; however much it be feared that the listlessness of non-labourers, and the fatigues of hard labourers, will continue to plead for the relief of intoxicating liquors, or exhilarating plants; one or other of which seem to have been in use in every age and country. As far as the use of Tobacco is a mere fashion or habit, commencing not only without but against a natural relish, and continued without the need of such a resort, your reasonings and warnings might reasonably be expected to be an overmatch for the pernicious indulgence. In every view your remedial efforts are highly meritorious, since they may check if they cannot cure the evil, and since a partial success may excite co-operating efforts which will gradually make it compleat: and I join heartily in every wish that such may be the result. At present Virginia is not much threatened with a speedy loss of her staple, whatever be the character really belonging, or ridiculously ascribed to it. Its culture is rather on the increase than the decline; owing to the disposition in Europe, particularly Great Britain to chew our Tobacco rather than eat our Wheat. This is not the best state of things either for them or us.

To Benjamin Waterhouse, 22 June 1822
DLC: Madison Papers

Treaty Powers

It is true that this branch [the House of Representatives] is not of necessity to be consulted in the forming of Treaties. But as its approbation and cooperation may often be necessary in carrying treaties into full effect; and as the support of the Government and of the plans of the President and Senate in general must be drawn from the purse which they hold, the sentiments of this body cannot fail to have very great weight, even when the body itself may have no constitutional authority.

To George Nicholas, 17 May 1788
PJM 11:48

The Union

WHO ARE ITS REAL FRIENDS? Not those who charge others with not being its friends, whilst their own conduct is wantonly multiplying its enemies. Not those who favor measures, which by pampering the spirit of speculation within and without the government, disgust the best friends of the Union. Not those who promote unnecessary accumulations of the debt of the Union, instead of the best means of discharging it as fast as possible; thereby encreasing the causes of corruption in the government, and the pretexts for new taxes under its authority, the former undermining the confidence, the latter alienating the affection of the people. Not those who study, by arbitrary interpretations and insidious precedents, to pervert the limited government of the Union, into a government of unlimited discretion, contrary to the will and subversive of the authority of the people.

National Gazette essay, 31 Mar. 1792
PJM 14:274

The Union of these States cannot in truth be too highly valued or too watchfully cherished. It is our best barrier against danger from without, and the only one against those armies and taxes, those wars and usurpations, which so readily grow out of the jealousies and ambition of neighbouring and independent States.

To the Chairman of the Republican
Society of Hancock County, Mass.,
15 Mar. 1809
PJM-PS 1:53

The advice nearest to my heart and deepest in my convictions is that the Union of the States be cherished and perpetuated. Let the open enemy to it be regarded as a Pandora with her box opened; and the disguised one, as the Serpent creeping with his deadly wiles into Paradise.

"Advice to My Country," 1834
DLC: Madison Papers

I am among those who are most anxious for the preservation of the Union of the States, and for the success of the constitutional experiment of which it is the basis. We owe it to ourselves and to the world, to watch, to cherish, and as far as possible, to perfect a new modification of the powers of Government, which aims at a better security against external danger, and internal disorder— a better provision for national strength and individual rights, than had been exemplified, under any previous form.

To Andrew Bigelow, 2 Apr. 1836
DLC: Madison Papers

Unity

In a government founded on the principles, and organized in the form, which distinguish that of the United States, discord alone, on points of vital importance, can render the nation weak in itself, or deprive it of that respect which guarantees its peace and security. With a union of its citizens, a government thus identified with the nation, may be considered as the strongest in the world; the participation of every individual in the rights and welfare of the whole, adding the greatest moral, to the greatest physical strength of which political society is susceptible.

To the Republican Meeting of Cecil
County, Md., 5 Mar. 1810
PJM-PS 2:263

Utopias

Mr. Owen's remedy for these vicissitudes [of the new industrial economy], implies that labour will be relished without the ordinary impulses to it; that the love of equality will supercede the desire of distinction; and that the increasing leisure from the improvements of machinery will promote intellectual cultivation, moral enjoyment, and innocent amusements, without any of the vicious resorts for the ennui of idleness. Custom is properly called a second nature. Mr. Owen makes it nature herself. His enterprize is nevertheless an interesting one. It will throw light on the maximum to which the force of education and habit can be carried; and like Helvetius's attempt to shew that all men come from the hand of nature perfectly equal, and owe every intellectual and moral difference, to the education of circumstances . . . will lead to a fuller sense of their great importance.

To Nicholas P. Trist, April 1827
DLC: Trist Papers

War

Whilst war is to depend on those whose ambition, whose revenge, whose avidity, or whose caprice may contradict the sentiment of the community, and yet be uncontrolled by it; whilst war is to be declared by those who are to spend the public money, not by those who are to pay it; by those who are to direct the public forces, not by those who are to support them; by those whose power is to be raised, not by those whose chains may be riveted, the disease must continue to be *hereditary* like the government of which it is the offspring. As the first step towards a cure, the government itself must be regenerated. Its will must be made subordinate to, or rather the same with, the will of the community.

National Gazette essay, 31 Jan. 1792
PJM 14:207

Of all the enemies to public liberty war is, perhaps, the most to be dreaded, because it comprises and develops the germ of every other. War is the parent of armies; from these proceed debts and taxes; and armies, and debts, and taxes are the known instruments for bringing the many under the domination of the few. In war, too, the discretionary power of the Executive is extended; its influence in dealing out offices, honors, and emoluments is multiplied; and all the means of seducing the minds, are added to those of subduing the force, of the people. The same malignant aspect in republicanism may be traced in the inequality of fortunes, and the opportunities of fraud, growing out of a state of war, and in the degeneracy of manners and of morals, engendered by both. No nation could preserve its freedom in the midst of continual warfare.

> *Political Observations*, 20 Apr. 1795
> *PJM* 15:518

War and Executive Power

Those who are to *conduct a war* cannot in the nature of things, be proper or safe judges, whether *a war ought* to be *commenced, continued*, or *concluded*. They are barred from the latter functions by a great principle in free government, analogous to that which separates the sword from the purse, or the power of executing from the power of enacting laws.

> *Helvidius* No. 1, 24 Aug. 1793
> *PJM* 15:71

War is in fact the true nurse of executive aggrandizement. In war a physical force is to be created, and it is the executive will which is to direct it. In war the public treasures are to be unlocked, and it is the executive hand which is to dispense them. In war the honors and emoluments of office are to be multiplied; and it is the executive patronage under which they are to be enjoyed. It is in war, finally, that laurels are to be gathered, and it is the executive brow they are to encircle. The strongest passions, and the most dangerous weaknesses of the human breast; ambition, avarice, vanity, the honorable or venial love of fame, are all in conspiracy against the desire and duty of peace.

> *Helvidius* No. 4, 14 Sept. 1793
> *PJM* 15:108

When a state of war becomes absolutely and clearly necessary, all good citizens will submit with alacrity to the calamities inseparable from it. But wars are so often the result of causes which prudence and a love of peace might obviate, that it is equally the duty and the characteristic of good citizens to keep a watchful, tho' not censorious eye, over that branch of the government which derives the greatest accession of power and importance from the armies, offices, and expences, which compose the equipage of war. In spite of all the claims and examples of patriotism, which ought by no means to be undervalued, the testimony of all ages forces us to admit, that war is among the most dangerous of all enemies to liberty; and that the executive is the most favored by it, of all the branches of power.

> "Political Reflections," 23 Feb. 1799
> *PJM* 17:241

George Washington

Death has robbed our country of its most distinguished ornament, and the world of one of its greatest benefactors. George Washington, the Hero of Liberty, the father of his Country, and the friend of man is no more. The General Assembly of his native state were ever the first to render him, living, the honors due to his virtues. They will not be the second, to pay to his memory the tribute of their tears.

> Speech in the Virginia General Assembly,
> 18 Dec. 1799
> *PJM* 17:295

Wine

The practicability and national economy of substituting to a great extent at least, for the foreign wines on which so large a sum is expended, those which can be produced at home, without withdrawing labour from objects not better rewarding it, is strongly illustrated by your experiments and statements; The introduction of a native wine is not a little recommended moreover, by its tendency to substitute a beverage favorable to temperate habits for the ardent liquors so destructive to the morals, the health, and the social happiness of the American people.

To John Adlum, 12 Apr. 1823
DLC: Madison Papers

Wisdom

A silly reason from a wise man is never the true one.

To Richard Rush, 27 June 1817
DLC: Madison Papers

The measures of wisdom are not seldom unlike its fabled Goddess; being neither matured at their birth, nor the offsprings of a single brain.

To Henry Lee, 31 Jan. 1825
DLC: Madison Papers

Women

The capacity of the female mind for studies of the highest order can not be doubted; having been sufficiently illustrated by its works of genius, of erudition and of Science. That it merits an improved system of education, comprizing a due reference to the condition and duties of female life, as distinguished from those of the other sex, must be as readily admitted. How far a collection of female Students into a public Seminary would be the best of plans for educating them, is a point on which different opinions may be expected to arise. Yours as the result of much observation on the youthful minds of females, and of long engagement in tutoring them, is entitled to great respect; and as experiment alone can fully decide the interesting problem, it is a justifiable wish that it may be made.

To Albert Picket, September 1821
DLC: Madison Papers

EPILOGUE

*It would be improper to close this communication without ex-
pressing a thankfulness, in which all ought to unite, for the numerous blessings with which our beloved Country, continues to
be favored; for the abundance which overspreads our land, and
the prevailing health of its inhabitants; for the preservation of
our internal tranquility, and the stability of our free institutions; and above all for the light of divine truth, and the protection of every man's conscience in the enjoyment of it.*

Annual Message to Congress, 7 Dec. 1813
DNA: Record Group 233, President's Messages

SUGGESTED READINGS

Any reader in search of James Madison would do well to begin with his correspondence. The ongoing modern edition of *The Papers of James Madison* (William T. Hutchinson and William M. E. Rachal, eds., Chicago and Charlottesville, Va., 1962–) provides complete and accurate, fully annotated transcripts of his papers, exhaustively indexed. The Congressional Series (17 vols.), running from 1751 to 1801, is completed. Two other series, the Secretary of State (3 vols.) and the Presidential (3 vols.), are ongoing. The Retirement Series has not yet been started. For the period of Madison's retirement, readers can refer to the last volume of Gaillard Hunt, ed., *The Writings of James Madison*, 9 vols. (New York, 1900–1910).

A guide to the most important Madison documents in print would include his notes on debates and speeches in the Continental Congress (*PJM*, vols. 2–7); Memorial and Remonstrance against Religious Assessments (ibid., 8:295–306); "Vices of the Political System of the United States" (ibid., 9:345–58); his essays for *The Federalist* (ibid., vol. 10); his speeches in the House of Representatives (ibid., vols. 11–16); his essays for the *National Gazette* (ibid., vol. 14); his *Helvidius* essays (ibid., vol. 15); the *Virginia Resolutions* and *The Report of 1800* (ibid., 17:185–91, 303–51); Madison's "Autobiography," *William and Mary Quarterly*, 3d ser., 2 (1945): 191–209; and his "Detached Memoranda," ibid., 3 (1946): 534–68.

A valuable one-volume compilation of Madison's writings is Marvin Meyers, ed., *The Mind of the Founder: Sources of the Political Thought of James Madison* (Hanover, N.H., 1981).

Those curious about the events at the Constitutional Convention will want to look at *Notes of Debates in the Federal Convention of 1787 Reported by James Madison,* introduced by Adrienne Koch (Athens, Ohio, 1966). And for those interested in the friendship between Madison and Thomas Jefferson, three elegant volumes of their letters have been edited by James Morton Smith as *The Republic of Letters: The Correspondence between Jefferson and Madison, 1776–1826,* 3 vols. (New York, 1995).

Biographies of Madison range from the sweeping and detailed six-volume *Life of James Madison* (Indianapolis, 1941–61) by Irving Brant to the brief but excellent study by Jack Rakove, *James Madison and the Creation of the American Republic* (Glenview, Ill., 1990). The best one-volume biography is by Ralph Ketcham, *James Madison: A Biography* (New York, 1971; rept. Charlottesville, Va., 1990). Robert A. Rutland's *James Madison: The Founding Father* (New York, 1987) is a short and very readable work.

Particular aspects of Madison's career have been studied as well. For Madison's intellectual preparation for the Constitutional Convention, see William Lee Miller, *The Business of May Next: James Madison and the Founding* (Charlottesville, Va., 1992). Madison's fifty-year friendship with Thomas Jefferson is the subject of Adrienne Koch's *Jefferson and Madison: The Great Collaboration* (New York, 1950). For a careful assessment of Madison's tenure as president, see Robert A. Rutland, *The Presidency of James Madison* (Lawrence, Kans., 1990). For a thorough study of Madison's conduct of the War of 1812, see J. C. A. Stagg, *Mr. Madison's War: Politics, Diplomacy, and Warfare in the Early American Republic, 1783–1830* (Princeton, N.J., 1983). And for a wonderfully written and engaging look at Madison's retirement years, see Drew R. McCoy, *The Last of the Fathers: James Madison and the Republican Legacy* (New York, 1989).

Finally, those readers interested in Madison's ideas should sample Drew R. McCoy, *The Elusive Republic: Political Economy in Jeffersonian America* (Chapel Hill, N.C., 1980), and especially

Lance Banning, *The Sacred Fire of Liberty: James Madison and the Creation of the Federal Republic, 1780–1792* (Ithaca, N.Y., 1995). For a critique of Madisonian liberalism, see Richard K. Matthews, *If Men Were Angels: James Madison and the Heartless Empire of Reason* (Lawrence, Kans., 1995).

INDEX

Speech (*see also* Press): freedom of, 99
Standing army, 44, 69, 100
States' rights, 31–35 (*see also* Federalism; Federal-state relations)
Stevenson, Andrew, 73, 97
Stuart, Archibald, 27, 78
Suffrage, 100

Talent, 16, 100
Taxation, 100, 101
Teackle, Littleton Dennis, 42
Term limits, 53, 101, 102 (*see also* Legislators; Legislatures)
Thomson, George, 42
Thruston, Buckner, 60
Tobacco, 103 (*see also* Drugs)
Torrey, Jesse, Jr., 66
Treaty powers, 103
Trist, Nicholas P.: letters to, 26, 48, 58, 59, 81, 83, 106
Truth, 51, 61

Unfair advantage, 62
Union, 22, 104, 105 (*see also* Constitution, U.S.)
United States: history of, 15; and intervention in foreign countries, 49; and politics, 14; and the world, 13
Unity, 105 (*see also* Union)
Utopias, 105

Verplanck, Gulian C., 42
Virginia, 11, 87, 88, 92, 94, 96; General Assembly of, 108; and tobacco, 103
Virginia, University of, 41, 89
Virginia Resolutions, 46, 48
Virtue, 12, 62, 95; and the people, 24

Walsh, Robert, Jr., 88, 96
War, 15, 38, 49, 50, 74, 100, 106; and executive power, 106, 107, 108
Washington, George, 1, 2, 108
Waterhouse, Benjamin, 103
Watterson, George, 38
Webster, Daniel, 28
Wine, 40, 72, 108
Wisdom, 109
Women, 42, 109
Wright, Francis, 99

CPSIA information can be obtained
at www.ICGtesting.com
Printed in the USA
FFOW04n2353090915
16634FF